PROPHECY

Thus Saith the Lord Thy God

Nadine Anderson

PublishAmerica
Baltimore

First printing

ISBN: 1-4137-5483-X
PUBLISHED BY PUBLISHAMERICA, LLLP
www.publishamerica.com
Baltimore

Printed in the United States of America

"Do not keep
the prophetic words
of this book
a secret."

ACKNOWLEDGMENTS

I give all the glory, honor and praise to God for the inspiration of this book. This book is the work of the Lord and it is good. It took three years of fasting and prayer to complete. But here it is, the word of God, live and direct, speaking to you.

INTRODUCTION

One day God asked me, "Daughter, why won't you prophesy to my people? I have given you my words and you have not spoken." Then the Lord took me through his word and asked me what I saw; then he commanded me to write what I saw and to publish it.

I have not prophecy to God's people because they would rather pay to hear a lie than the truth for free. The people of God have itching ears and have gone astray after Balaam. The people of God have sold themselves to the enemy for nothing, without price. To those wonderful saints who are constantly seeking a word from God, here is a volume of words for your satisfaction.

Sometimes I feel like Jeremiah when the word of the Lord comes to me. I am deeply troubled when God's people will not hear the voice of their God; I am deeply wounded when they rebel against God as the people of old. But the Lord is their stay and he is still in love with his people and continues to call out unto them to change and amend their wicked ways before it's too late.

The people stone the prophets of God in their hearts, crucify them with their tongues and secretly plot their death when they declare the word of the Lord unto them. But all is well, because their reward is not with man but with God, and God stands watch over his words to bring them to pass. God declares, touch not my anointed nor do my prophets no harm for I have rebuked kings for their sake and I will repay every man according to his deeds.

In the volume of this book is the word of God and He is speaking, I beg you to hear Him, to listen to Him and to obey Him. Do not be like the deaf adder that stoppeth her ears from hearing. But be a wise child with a hearing ear to hear what the spirit of the Lord is saying.

A tip from a prophet, always seek a sure word from the mouth of God for yourself, for there are many false prophets amongst you.

It is my prayer that as you read this book you will be aware that God is speaking to you in the volume of his words. I pray that your salvation is established and secure. I pray that you seek after righteousness at all cost and experience the revelation of God's word for your life. I pray that you will remember the laws of God and be directed to correction and experience God's intimate fellowship. I pray that you will have a magnified view of marriage and relationship with man and God. I pray that your enemies will be at peace with you and your sins will be no more remembered. Amen.

CONTENTS

PROPHECY
THUS SAITH THE LORD
Part 1

1. You shall live and not die to declare the glory of God.
2. Thy faith has made thee whole.
3. I the Lord, will prosper you and make you very, very wealthy.
4. I am the Lord; I will heal thee because you have trusted me.
5. I am the Lord that healeth thee of all thy diseases.
6. I am the author and finisher of your faith, so believe in me and nothing shall be impossible unto you.
7. I created the heavens and the earth, what can I not do for you.
8. You were dead but now you shall live.
9. You were lost but I have found you and surnamed you as my own.
10. I chastise you because I love you and you are my own.
11. I will never leave you nor forsake you.
12. I will make you as my battle axe and use you as an instrument of war.
13. When I call, you will hear and where I send you, you will go.
14. Go in peace, no evil will befall thee, I have angels watching over thee.
15. I have anointed you to preach my words to my flock.
16. I have called thee to preach to the Gentiles and the Greeks.
17. I have gone before thee to make the crooked path straight.
18. I will perfect everything that concerneth thee.
19. You are the light of the world, draw men unto me.

20. God cannot lie, so believe him.
21. You were barren but now you shall bear much fruit.
22. I have a hedge of protection around you that no man shall harm you.
23. You were up, now you are down, I will lift you high and mighty above your foes.
24. You will not cast your young before time, but will bring forth in due season.
25. I have rent you, now I will mend you and cause you to be glorious.
26. The time is short, the time is now, arise and go forth.
27. Stand still and see the salvation of the Lord.
28. Don't faint my child for there is a blessing in the storm.
29. People will come and people will go but I will never leave you.
30. You were young and now you are old, God has never forsaken you.
31. The Lord will bless you with a seed and multiply your harvest.
32. Before you were born I knew your name and called you my very own.
33. You will find a place of rest in the arms of God.
34. Little children humble yourselves and draw near.
35. Come my beloved and walk with me all the day.
36. If I am God, believe all my words and cast your bread upon the waters.
37. The Lord hears for He is not deaf and the Lord sees for He is not blind.
38. When you call I will answer thee and when you cry I will comfort thee.
39. If it were not so I would have told you but it is so, now believe and receive my promises for your life.
40. I sit high and I look low, there is nothing that is unseen from my eyes.
41. I have called you a prophet, why will you not prophecy my words to my people?
42. The time is short and the days are swiftly passing by so come up higher.

43. Low, I have behold him and seen the beauty that is within him.
44. No weapons formed against me shall prosper.
45. God will be your defense and an high tower.
46. No man can curse you for the Lord your God has called you blessed.
47. I will bless those who bless you and curse those who curse you.
48. Nations shall flee at your presence and turn from their wicked ways.
49. What I have in store for you is more than your mind can imagine.
50. I have called you daughter and I have called you son, now I call you friend.
51. Because you have loved me and have obeyed me I will cause blessings to overtake you.
52. You have kept the faith in spite of disappointment, rejection and destruction, now I will build thee and you shall be built.

THUS SAITH THE LORD
Part 2

1. They are gone over the passage.
2. The high ones of stature shall be hewn down.
3. The haughty shall be humbled.
4. Thou shall make you of a quick study.
5. With the breath of your lips shall you slay the wicked.
6. I will cause a child to lead them.
7. The gentiles will seek you for my glory is seen upon you.
8. That which I have spoken shall come to pass.
9. That which I have spoken unto you shall manifest.
10. If you praise me I will cut off your adversaries.
11. The children of your enemies shall obey you.
12. I will make a way out of nowhere for you.
13. Trust God and be not afraid.
14. Declare my doing among the people.
15. I will make you more precious than fine gold.
16. Her time is near to come, and her days shall not be prolonged.
17. I will set you in your own land.
18. I will give thee rest from thy sorrow, fear and bondage.
19. The staff of the wicked have I broken and the scepter of the rulers.
20. The seed of evil doers shall never be renowned.
21. Surely as I have thought, so shall it come to pass.
22. As I have purposed so shall it stand.
23. In the night I will lay waste your enemies and bring them to silence.

24. Let mine outcasts dwell with thee.
25. Take counsel and execute my judgment.
26. He is very proud but his lies shall not be so.
27. It shall come to pass.
28. He shall come to his sanctuary to pray.
29. He shall not prevail against you.
30. Within three years it shall be so.
31. Thou shall plant pleasant plants.
32. God shall rebuke them.
33. You shall chased them as the chaff before the wind.
34. They shall be confounded.
35. I have set a perverse spirit in the midst of thee.
36. Vow a vow unto the Lord and perform it.
37. I will make you a blessing in the midst of the land.
38. A grievous vision is declared unto me.
39. The treacherous dealer dealeth treacherously.
40. Go, set a watchman and let him declare what he seeth.
41. The morning cometh and also the night.
42. Within a year all the glory of your enemy shall fail.
43. It is a day of trouble, and of treading down and perplexity.
44. Thy choicest valleys shall be full of chariots.
45. The horsemen shall set themselves in array at the gate.
46. You have not looked to your maker to solve your problems.
47. Behold joy and gladness cometh.
48. This iniquity shall not be purged from you till you die.
49. I will clothe you, give you strength and power to do my will.
50. I will give you the keys to open doors and to shut doors.
51. Her own feet will carry her afar off to sojourn.
52. Make sweet melody; sing many songs to be remembered.

THUS SAITH THE LORD
Part 3

1. Thy brother shall rise again.
2. Believest thou this.
3. Many will say you have a devil and should not be heard.
4. The works I do in my father's name bears witness of me.
5. Many will believe on you where I will send you.
6. The Lord has come to awake you from your sleep.
7. Now, the true worshippers shall worship me in spirit and truth.
8. God is a spirit; worship him in spirit and truth.
9. I perceive that you are a prophet.
10. Go call your husband and come unto me.
11. You must finish the work of your father.
12. The field is ripe with her harvest.
13. The reapers are paid their hire.
14. You will rejoice for sowing and reaping in the vineyard.
15. You have sown but another reapeth the fields.
16. Now you will reap where you have not sown.
17. Faint not, for your labor unto God is not invain.
18. You must decrease so that the Holy Spirit will increase upon you.
19. If you believe in Jesus, how can you perish?
20. God who is mighty in love has rescued you from sin and death.
21. The miracles you do is because God is with you.
22. If you are not born of water and of the spirit, I know you not.
23. If you are born of the flesh you are of the devil.
24. If you are born of the spirit you are of God.

25. Be not surprise you must be born again.
26. I am the voice of one crying in the wilderness.
27. Every purpose is established by counsel.
28. Come and see if anything good can come out of Nazareth.
29. Make straight the way of the Lord.
30. I will send you but your own will not receive you.
31. Wait on God and pray until I give you power from heaven.
32. You must suffer many things for the glory of God to be revealed in you.
33. Your eyes will be opened and you will see Jesus.
34. Your understanding will be opened and you will know the scripture.
35. You will receive your due rewards for your deeds.
36. Weep not for me, but for yourself and your children.
37. I will cause the voices of your enemies to prevail against you for my glory.
38. Beware, they will chose the ways of the world over my words.
39. Make your house a house of prayer.
40. Your enemies will serve you and you will crush them.
41. Cast your identity upon Jesus.
42. You shall give birth to a son for the service of the Lord.
43. He is risen.
44. You must save others but yourself God will save.
45. Walk in my commandments and my ordinance.
46. Go into all the nations and preach the gospel to all people.
47. You are rich.
48. The Lord is your covering.
49. Hear what the spirit of the Lord is saying.
50. Cast not away your confidence in the Lord.
51. You must live by faith to please God.
52. Walk by faith and not by sight as do the blinds.
53. I will pour out my spirit upon you and magnify your name.
54. By faith every obstacles will be removed and your enemies destroyed.

THUS SAITH THE LORD
Part 4

1. I will make the land desolate because they have committed a trespass.
2. Woe unto the foolish prophets that follow their own spirit, and have seen nothing.
3. They have seen vanity and lying divination.
4. I the Lord have not spoken.
5. My hands shall be upon the prophets that see vanity and divine lies.
6. My child the lying prophets have seduced you. Woe to them.
7. I the Lord will discover the foundation of liars and expose them.
8. The witches that hunt the souls of my people to slay them will know that I am the Lord.
9. You have idols in you heart, yet you seek my council.
10. Repent and turn your hearts from your idols and seek me.
11. I the Lord will answer you myself if you seek me with idols in your hearts.
12. I the Lord have deceived the prophet and will destroy him.
13. When you sin I will send a famine to cut you off.
14. They shall come forth and you will see their ways and doings.
15. For I do nothing without cause or purpose.
16. When I saw you polluted in your blood I spoke life to you.
17. Behold this is the time of love and I will cover you.
18. I am in covenant with you for you are mines.
19. I have cleanse you and anointed you with oil.
20. I have clothed you in the best and will dress you in royalty.

21. Thou shalt be as my mouth. (God's mouthpiece)
22. Do not listen to the words of the false prophets.
23. They shall come with speed swiftly.
24. If ye will not believe, surely ye shall not be established.
25. Let him make speed, and hasten his work.
26. Whom shall I send, and who will go for us?
27. And his heart was moved.
28. Take heed, and be quiet, fear not, neither be fainthearted.
29. They have taken evil counsel against you.
30. It shall not stand; neither shall it come to pass.
31. Ask thee a sign of the Lord thy God.
32. It shall come to pass in that day.
33. They shall come.
34. He shall come up over all his channels, and go over all his banks.
35. He shall overflow and go over.
36. They take evil counsel together, and it shall come to nothing.
37. The word of evil sent against you shall not stand.
38. The Lord shall be a gin and a snare unto your enemies.
39. Your enemies shall stumble, fall, taken, broken and ensnared.
40. The diviners shall be driven to darkness.
41. This battle shall be with the burning of fire.
42. War with confused noise and dress in red garments.
43. They shall devour Israel with open mouth.
44. The Lord has sent a word into you for a light.
45. The iniquity workers have been driven to madness.
46. Every one is a hypocrite and an evildoer.
47. They rob the fatherless and the widows.
48. I will send you against an hypocritical nation.
49. I tread them down like the mire of the streets.
50. My hands have found the riches of the people.
51. I have removed thy bounds and given thee treasures of darkness.
52. My anointing has destroyed the yoke and burden upon you.

THUS SAITH THE LORD
Part 5

1. She shall turn her to her hire.
2. Her merchandise and her hire shall be holiness to the Lord.
3. It shall not be treasured nor laid up.
4. Your merchandise shall be for them that dwell before the Lord.
5. The curse devoured the earth.
6. Strong drink shall be bitter to them that drink it.
7. The city of confusion is broken down.
8. The gate is smitten with destruction.
9. They shall lift up their voice.
10. The treacherous dealers have dealt very treacherously.
11. Fear, and the pit, and the snare, are upon thee.
12. The windows from on high are open.
13. The foundations of the earth do shake.
14. They shall be shut up in the prison.
15. After many days shall they be visited.
16. It shall never be built.
17. Thou shalt bring down the noise of strangers.
18. We have waited for him.
19. The foot shall tread it down.
20. Let favor be shown to the wicked.
21. They will not see.
22. The fire in thine enemies shall devour them.
23. They are dead, they shall not live, they are deceased, and they shall not rise.
24. Thou have removed it far unto all the ends of the earth.

25. You are with child and in pain to bring forth deliverance.
26. Thy dead men shall live and your dead body shall arise.
27. He shall slay the dragon that is in the sea.
28. I the Lord do keep it.
29. I will keep it night and day.
30. Who would set the briers and thorns against me in battle?
31. Israel shall blossom and bud and fill the world with fruits.
32. The groves and images shall not stand up.
33. The woman came, and set them on fire.
34. I will not have mercy on them.
35. Woe to the crown of pride.
36. The priest and the prophet have erred through strong drink.
37. They err in vision, they stumble in judgment.
38. There shall be heaviness and sorrow.
39. I will camp against thee round about.
40. Thy voice shall be as of one that hath a familiar spirit.
41. Yes, it shall be at an instant suddenly.
42. Your tribulation shall be as a dream of a night vision.
43. His soul hath appetite.
44. I have poured out the spirit of deep sleep and closed your eyes.
45. I have covered the prophets, the rulers and the seers with sleep.
46. Read the word of the books I have given thee.
47. This people draw near with their mouth and words but not their hearts.
48. They have removed their hearts far from me.
49. The deaf shall hear the words of the book.
50. The eyes of the blind shall see out of obscurity and darkness.
51. The scorner is consumed.
52. All that watch for iniquity are cut off.

THUS SAITH THE LORD
Part 6

1. You shall not now be ashamed.
2. They shall sanctify my name.
3. They that erred in spirit shall come to understanding.
4. Woe to the rebellious children.
5. They will carry their riches in new cars and their treasures in trucks unto you.
6. Their strength is to sit still.
7. Write what I have told you and put it in a book for a remembrance.
8. They are lying children who will not harken unto my laws.
9. They are a rebellious people.
10. Say to the seers, see not.
11. Say to the prophets, prophecy not truth, prophecy deceits.
12. Get out of the way and remove yourself.
13. In quietness and in confidence shall you be strong.
14. You shall be blessed if you wait upon the Lord.
15. Thou shall weep no more.
16. When he hears your voice, he will answer thee.
17. He will be very gracious unto thee at thy crying.
18. I have given thee the bread of adversity and water of affliction.
19. This is the way, walk in the path I have set before you.
20. You shall defile the covering of graven images of silver and molten images of gold.
21. You shall cast graven images away as menstrual cloth.
22. Thou shall say unto it, get thee hence.
23. I will give you rain for the seeds you have sown.

24. I will cause the increase of your ground to be plentiful.
25. The towers shall fall.
26. I will bind up the breach of my people.
27. I will heal the stroke of your wound for a testimony.
28. I know you are burning with anger but cease from it.
29. Your burden is heavy and I will give you relief.
30. I have made your tongue a devouring fire.
31. I will give you a song to sing.
32. Your enemies shall be beaten down with the voice of God.
33. He hath made it deep and large.
34. He will bring evil and will not call back his words.
35. Behold, a leader shall lead my people in righteousness.
36. I will cause the blind to see and the deaf to hear.
37. Your stammering tongue shall speak plainly.
38. The vile person shall no more be called liberal.
39. Trust him not for his heart will work iniquity.
40. They seek opportunity to practice hypocrisy against you.
41. He uses wicked devices to destroy the poor with lying words.
42. Your careless daughters must hear my words.
43. Arise and remove yourself from ease.
44. They shall abandon the palaces for your possession.
45. I will cause you to dwell in a peaceful place of quite rest.
46. Blessed are you for you have sown beside all waters.
47. They shall not deal treacherously with thee anymore.
48. Woe unto them that have spoiled thee of thy blessings.
49. Your spoil shall be gathered back unto you.
50. Shutteth your eyes from seeing evil.
51. I will give thee bread and guarantee thee water.
52. I will show you the land that is afar off that I have promised.

THUS SAITH THE LORD
Part 7

1. Not one of the stakes shall be removed neither any cords broken.
2. I will cause the lame to take the prey.
3. Thy tacklings are loosed.
4. I shall forgive you of your iniquity.
5. You will not say I am sick anymore.
6. Come nearer and hear what I have to say to you.
7. I have utterly destroyed them.
8. I have delivered them to the slaughter.
9. My sword is filled with the blood of thine enemies.
10. Today is the day of the Lord's vengeance.
11. This is the year of recompence for Zion.
12. Read and seek ye out of the book of the Lord knowledge.
13. They shall see the glory of the Lord.
14. Be strong, fear not for God is with thee.
15. The lame shall walk and the dumb speak.
16. A way and an highway shall be there.
17. It shall not be found there.
18. Sorrow and sighing shall flee away.
19. In the highway of the fullers field you will find deliverance.
20. What confidence is this wherein thou trustest.
21. That which you speak are vain words.
22. I have given thee counsel and strength for war.
23. Why do you rebel against me?
24. Ye shall worship before this alter.
25. Now therefore give pledges unto the Lord.

26. I will give thee two thousand horses.
27. Go up against this land, and destroy it.
28. I have sent you to the men that sit upon the walls.
29. Let not the prophet deceive you.
30. I will surely deliver you from all your enemies.
31. Make no agreement with thine enemies nor come out to meet them.
32. Drink water from your own cistern.
33. Hold your peace and answer your adversary not a word.
34. The children are come to birth but there is no strength to bring forth.
35. This day is a day of trouble, rebuke and blasphemy.
36. Lift up your prayers for the remnant that is left.
37. Be not afraid of the words that thou hast heard.
38. Behold, I will send a blast upon him.
39. I will cause him to fall by the sword in his own hand.
40. He is come forth to make war with thee.
41. You will receive a letter with a message, read it.
42. The virgin, the daughter of Zion, hath despised thee.
43. The daughter of Jerusalem hath shaken her head at thee.
44. I will cut down the tall cedars and choice fir trees.
45. I will enter into the heights of his border.
46. I have formed it, now I have brought it to pass.
47. I know thy coming in and thy going out.
48. I know thy rage against me.
49. You shall eat this year such as groweth of itself.
50. Take not downward and bear fruit upward.
51. He shall not come into this city nor shoot an arrow there.
52. Behold early in the morning they will all be dead corpes.

THUS SAITH THE LORD
Salvation

1. It is God's power to save all who believe.
2. He is trying to lead you to repent.
3. God will give glory, honor and peace to all who do what is good.
4. You are confident that you are a guide for the blind.
5. You are a light for those who are in darkness.
6. You are an instructor for the foolish.
7. You are a teacher for the ignorant.
8. Why should I still be condemned as a sinner?
9. God brings the dead to life.
10. God speak into being what did not exist.
11. Because of our sin He was given over to die for our salvation.
12. While, we were yet sinners, Christ died for us.
13. By his blood, we are now put right with God.
14. We were God's enemies, but He made us his friends through Christ.
15. Everyone has sinned.
16. God's grace is much greater than anything else.
17. We have died to sin. So also we might live a new life.
18. For when we die, we are set free from the power of sin.
19. Sin has no power over him.
20. Sin must no longer rule in your mortal bodies.
21. Give yourself to God.
22. Don't surrender any part of yourself to sin for wicked purposes.
23. Sin must not be your master.
24. You do not live under the law but under grace.

25. But thanks be to God.
26. Your gain is a life fully dedicated to God.
27. God's free gift is eternal life.
28. But in the new way of the spirit.
29. There is no condemnation now for those who live in Christ.
30. To be controlled by the spirit results in life and peace.
31. You live as the spirit tells you to.
32. Whoever doesn't have the spirit of Christ does not belong to him.
33. If Christ lives in you, the spirit is life for you.
34. You will live.
35. Those who are led by God's spirit are God's children.
36. The spirit makes you God's children.
37. We will posses the blessings he keeps for his people.
38. We will also share his glory.
39. God will freely give us all things.
40. Who can separate us from the love of Christ?
41. Nothing or no one can separate us from the love of Christ.
42. In all things we have complete victory through Christ.
43. I am certain nothing can separate us from God's love.
44. I am speaking the truth, I belong to Christ and I do not lie.
45. They have the true worship.
46. They have received God's promise.
47. For we are the people he called.
48. I will call my people.
49. Yet only a few of them will be saved.
50. God's message is near you, on your lips and in your heart.
51. We preach the message of faith.
52. You will be saved.
53. It is by our confession that we are saved.
54. We believe in our heart and confess with our mouth.

THE SAINTS OF THE LORD

1. But not all have accepted the good news.
2. The message comes through preaching Christ.
3. Faith comes from hearing the message.
4. I was found by those who were not looking for me.
5. I appeared to those who were not asking for me.
6. All day long I held out my hands to welcome a disobedient and rebellious people.
7. It is the same way now.
8. His choice is based on his grace.
9. It will be life for the dead.
10. The savior will come from Zion.
11. Let us stop doing the things that belongs to the dark.
12. God has accepted that person.
13. We each should firmly make up our own minds.
14. We do not live for ourselves only.
15. We do not die for ourselves only.
16. If we live it is for the Lord we live.
17. If we die it is for the Lord we die.
18. Whether we live or die, we belong to the Lord.
19. They became Christians before I did.

RIGHTEOUSNESS
The Right to Serve God

1. I am chosen and called by God to preach the Good News.
2. He was shown with great power.
3. You teach others, why don't you teach yourself?
4. You preach, do not steal yet you steal.
5. You say do not commit adultery but you commit adultery.
6. You detest idols but you rob temples.
7. Who is a real Christian?
8. A real Christian is real on the inside.
9. God must be true.
10. There is not one who is righteous.
11. In the past God was patient and over looked the sins of his people.
12. In the present time God deals with the sins of his people.
13. A person is put right with God only though faith.
14. Because of his faith God accepted him as righteous.
15. God accepted him as righteous.
16. For we are God's friends.
17. The promise was based on faith.
18. His faith did not leave him.
19. He did not doubt God's promise.
20. His faith filled him with power.
21. He gave praise to God.
22. He was sure God would be able to do what he had promised.
23. Jesus was raised to life in order to put us right with God.
24. But the two are not the same.
25. Surrender yourself to God to be used for righteous purposes.

26. The spirit is life for you because you are in right standing with God.
27. Those he called, he put right with himself.
28. He shared his glory with them.
29. Who will accuse God's chosen people?
30. God himself declared his people not guilty.
31. I promised you righteousness.
32. The Lord will settle his account with the world shortly.
33. Who can explain his decisions?
34. Who can understand his ways?
35. Offer yourself as a living sacrifice to God.
36. Do not conform yourselves to the standards of this world.
37. Then will you be able to know the will of God.
38. Share your belongings with your needy fellow Christians.
39. Work hard and do not be lazy.
40. Open your homes to strangers.
41. Ask God to bless those who persecute you.
42. Try to do what everyone considers to be good.
43. Never take revenge but instead let God's anger do it.
44. If your enemies are hungry, feed them.
45. If your enemies are thirsty give him drink.
46. Do not let evil defeat you; instead conquer evil with good.
47. You must obey the authorities.
48. Be under obligation to no one.
49. Let us take up weapons for fighting in the light.
50. Take up the weapons of the Lord Jesus Christ.
51. You should decide never to do anything to cause others to stumble or fall to sin.
52. I follow Christ.
53. Christ has been divided into groups.
54. He sent me to tell the good news.

REVELATION
THE KNOWLEDGE OF GOD
Part 1

1. By her teaching she misleads my servants.
2. You tolerate that woman Jezebel who calls herself a messenger of God.
3. I have given her time to repent of her sins.
4. She does not want to turn from her immorality.
5. I will also kill her followers.
6. I am the one who knows everyone's thoughts and wishes.
7. I will repay each of you according to what you have done.
8. I will not put any other burden on you.
9. I will give you the same authority I received from my father.
10. I will give them authority over the nations to rule them.
11. Listen to what the spirit of the Lord is saying.
12. They will be imprisoned for revealing the word of Christ.
13. Write down the things I will show you and publish them.
14. I have authority over death and the world of the dead.
15. I know what you have done.
16. I know how hard you have worked and how patient you have been.
17. I know that you cannot tolerate evil people.
18. You are patient and have suffered for my sake and have not given up.
19. You do not love me now as you did at first.
20. Think how far you have fallen.
21. Turn from your sins and do what you did at first.

22. I know your troubles.
23. I know that you are poor, but really you are rich.
24. I know the evil things said about you by those who claim to Christians.
25. Don't be afraid of anything you are about to suffer.
26. The devil will put you to the test.
27. I know where you live.
28. You are true to me and did not abandon your faith.
29. There are a few things I have against you.
30. There are some among you who follow the teaching of Balaam.
31. Turn from your sin, if you don't, I will come to you quickly.
32. I know your love, your faithfulness, your service and your patience.
33. I know that you are doing more now than you did at first.
34. Wake up and strengthen what you still have before it dies.
35. I know what you are doing.
36. I know that you think you are alive but I say you are dead.
37. A few of you have kept your white garments clean.
38. I will come upon you like a thief.
39. I know that you have a little power.
40. I have closed the doors and no man will open.
41. I have opened the door in front of you, walk through it.
42. I have opened a door that no man can close.
43. I will make them come and bow down at your feet.
44. They will all know that I love you.
45. You have kept my commandments and endured.
46. I will keep you safe from the time of trouble.
47. I am coming soon.
48. I know that you are neither cold nor hot.
49. Because you are lukewarm, I will vomit you from my mouth.
50. You say I am rich and well off, beware.
51. I have all I need.
52. You are miserable and pitiful.
53. Cover-up your shameful nakedness.
54. I rebuke and punish all whom I love.

THE KNOWLEDGE OF GOD
Part 2

1. I saw an open door in heaven.
2. Come up here and I will show you what is to come.
3. The spirit took control of me.
4. You will cry bitterly because no one will be found worthy.
5. They shall sing a new song.
6. They shall rule on the earth.
7. You are worthy to receive power, wealth, wisdom and strength.
8. I will cause you to ride out as a conqueror to conquer.
9. He was given a large sword.
10. Rest a little while longer.
11. Salvation comes from God, who sits on the throne.
12. Never again will they hunger and thirst for they have drank living water.
13. God will wipe every tear from your eyes.
14. A Third of the ships will be destroyed.
15. The name of the star is bitterness.
16. Then I looked and saw an eagle flying high in the air.
17. They will seek death, but will not find it.
18. They will want to die but death will flee from them.
19. I heard the noise of many horses rushing into battle.
20. The first horror is over.
21. I saw the horses and their riders.
22. They did not stop worshiping demons.
23. They did not repent of their hatred and their murders.
24. They did not repent of their magic.

25. They did not repent of their sexual immorality.
26. They did not repent of their stealing.
27. As soon as they spoke, I wrote.
28. Do not write it down.
29. There will be no more delay.
30. God will accomplish his secret plans.
31. Take it and eat it, sweet as honey but bitter as gall.
32. You must preach God's message to many nations, race, language and kings.
33. They have authority to shut up the sky.
34. He will defeat and kill them.
35. As their enemies watched, they went up into heaven as a cloud.
36. The second horror is over.
37. The third horror will come soon.
38. The time has come to reward your servants, the prophets.
39. She was soon to give birth.
40. The pains and suffering of childbirth made her cry out.
41. He stood in front of the woman.
42. She was soon to give birth.
43. She gave birth to a son.
44. The woman fled to a place God had prepared for her.
45. Then war broke out in heaven.
46. The dragon was defeated and cast out of heaven.
47. The dragon, the ancient serpent named the devil or Satan.
48. Now God's salvation has come.
49. Now God has shown his power as king.
50. Now his messiah has shown his authority.
51. They won the victory by the blood of Jesus and their testimonies.
52. The devil has come down to you.
53. The devil pursued the woman who had given birth to the boy.
54. She was given two wings of a large eagle to fly away.

THE KNOWLEDGE OF GOD
Part 3

1. She will be taken care of for three and a half years.
2. Who is like the beast?
3. It began to curse God.
4. This second beast performed great miracles.
5. No one could buy or sell without the mark of the beast.
6. The number of the beast is 666, the number of man.
7. They that receive the number of the beast are condemned.
8. The time has come for God to judge all people of the earth.
9. Honor God and praise his greatness.
10. She has fallen.
11. Great Babylon has fallen.
12. Happy are those who die in the service of the Lord.
13. Use your sickle and reap the harvest.
14. But, they would not turn from their sins.
15. They did not turn from their evil ways.
16. They are the spirits of demons that perform miracles.
17. Happy is he who stays awake and guards his clothes.
18. It is done.
19. All the islands disappeared.
20. All the mountains vanished.
21. When I saw her, I was completely amazed.
22. They will take away everything she has and leave her naked.
23. She is now haunted by demons and unclean spirits.
24. All kinds of unclean spirits live in her.
25. All kinds of filthy and hateful birds live in her.

26. Come out my people! Come out from her.
27. You must not take part in her sin.
28. You must not share in her punishment.
29. God remembers her wicked ways.
30. Treat her exactly as she has treated you.
31. Pay her back double for all she has done for you.
32. Here I sit a queen, I will never know grief.
33. She will be burned with fire.
34. She will be struck with plagues, disease, grief and famine in one day.
35. In just one hour you have been punished.
36. They stand a long way off.
37. All your wealth and glamour are gone.
38. You will never find them again.
39. She used to dress herself.
40. In one hour she lost everything.
41. In one hour she lost all of her wealth.
42. All the good things you longed to own have disappeared.
43. For God has condemned her for what she did to you.
44. With your false magic you deceived all the people of the world.
45. God has punished her because she killed his servants.
46. For the time has come for the wedding of the lamb.
47. The bride has prepared herself for the marriage.
48. His rider is called faithful and true.
49. His eyes were like a flame of fire.
50. He had a name written on him.
51. The robe he wore was covered with blood.
52. Out of his mouth came a sharp sword.
53. Come and eat the flesh of kings.
54. The false prophets who had performed miracles are dead.

THE KNOWLEDGE OF GOD
Part 4

1. Don't do it.
2. Lock and seal it.
3. They came to life and ruled.
4. The second death has no power over them.
5. They shall be priest of God.
6. Satan will be set loose from his prison.
7. Satan will bring them all together for battle.
8. Fire came down from heaven and destroyed them.
9. You will be tormented day and night forever and ever.
10. The devil was thrown into the lake of fire and sulfur.
11. Books were opened.
12. Then the sea gave up its dead.
13. The lake of fire is the second death.
14. All sinners will be thrown in the lake of fire.
15. The New Jerusalem.
16. You are prepared like a bride dress and ready to meet her husband.
17. Now God's home is with people.
18. He will live with them.
19. They shall be his people.
20. There will be no more death.
21. The old things have disappeared.
22. Now I will make all things new.
23. These words are true and can be trusted.
24. They will be my children.
25. They will be my people.

26. Come and I will show you the bride, the wife of the lamb.
27. The angel carried me to the top of a very high mountain.
28. The kings of the earth will bring their wealth into your house.
29. They will never be closed.
30. The wealth of the nations will be brought into your city.
31. Once each month.
32. They will see his face.
33. It's leaves are for the healing of the nations.
34. They will rule as kings forever.
35. Listen, says Jesus, I am coming soon.
36. Happy are those who obey the prophetic words.
37. Do not keep the prophetic words of this book a secret.
38. The time is near when all things will happen.
39. Whoever is evil must go on doing evil.
40. Whoever is filthy must go on being filthy.
41. Whoever is good must go on doing good.
42. Whoever is holy must go on being holy.
43. I will bring my rewards with me.
44. I, Jesus have sent my angels to announce things to come.
45. The spirit and the bride say come.
46. Come, whoever is thirsty.
47. Accept the water of life as a gift.
48. It's for whomever wants it.
49. Yes indeed, I am coming soon.
50. So be it come Lord Jesus.
51. I am finish hearing and seeing them.
52. I was about to worship angels, but he stopped me.
53. I am a servant together with thee.
54. I am the first and the last.

REMEMBERANCE
THE LAWS OF GOD
Part 1

1. Hear the commandments of the Lord.
2. Keep the laws of God and practice them.
3. Teach the laws of God unto your children diligently.
4. Place the laws of God upon the walls of your house.
5. Obey God's laws, statues, and judgments.
6. The Lord has delivered me from captivity and bondage.
7. Thou shall have no other god's before me.
8. Thou shall not make unto thee any graven images.
9. Make no likeness of anything in the earth or the waters.
10. Make no likeness of anything that is in the heaven above.
11. Thou shall not worship any other god, for I am a jealous God.
12. I will bring your iniquity upon your children of four generations.
13. Thou shall not use God's name invain.
14. Keep the Sabbath day holy a day of rest in the Lord.
15. Six days shall thou labour and do all thy work.
16. Honour thy father and thy mother that it will be well with thee.
17. Thou shall not kill.
18. Thou shall not commit adultery. (Sleep with another mate)
19. Thou shall not steal.
20. Thou shall not lie.
21. Thou shall not purgery thyself.
22. Thou shall not lust after thy neighbor.
23. Thou shall not covet or envy they neighbor.

24. Thou shall love the Lord thy God with all thine heart.
25. Thou shall serve the Lord thy God.
26. Observe and do the commandments of the Lord.
27. Believe in God and believe his prophets.
28. Do the will of God for your life.
29. Walk in the pathway of righteousness.
30. Deny not God and he will not deny you.
31. Suffer all things for the gospel.
32. Repent when you fall into sin.
33. Love your enemies, don't hate them.
34. Bless those that curse you.
35. Forgive every one of all things.
36. Profane not the temple of God.
37. Be faithful unto God and your service to him.
38. Be sincere to God and man.
39. Show mercy to all men.
40. Praise God for his goodness, mercy and grace.
41. Forsake practicing sorcerery.
42. Swear not against heaven or earth.
43. Tempt not God.
44. Read the word of the Lord.
45. Hide the words of God in your heart.
46. Sin not against God.
47. Trust God and have faith in God.
48. Believe God in all things for he cannot lie.
49. Love the Lord God with all thine heart, mind, soul and body.
50. Obey the voice of God and the word of the Lord Almighty.
51. Give freely as you have received freely.
52. Love all man and show charity at all times.
53. Seek the Lord with all thine heart and with all thy soul.
54. Harken unto the voice of the Lord diligently.

THE LAWS OF GOD
Part 2

1. It's an abomination to commit incest.
2. It's an abomination for man to lie with man.
3. It's an abomination for woman to lie with woman.
4. It's an abomination for mankind to lie with beast.
5. Man shall not wear women's clothing.
6. It's an abomination for man to wear women's undergarment.
7. Woman shall not wear men's clothing.
8. It's and abomination for women to wear men's clothing.
9. Homosexuality is an abomination.
10. The practice of witchcraft and sorcerery is an abomination.
11. Putting anything and anyone before God is idolatry.
12. Idolatry is an abomination.
13. Filth and perversion is an abomination.
14. Whoredom is an abomination.
15. Profaning the name of God is an abomination.
16. Giving your children to the fire gods is an abomination.
17. Communication with familiar spirits is an abomination.
18. A woman with a familiar spirit must be put to death.
19. A man with a familiar spirit must be put to death.
20. A wizard shall surely be put to death.
21. A witch must not be permitted to live.
22. Blaspheming the name of God is an abomination.
23. He that killeth must be put to death.
24. The murderer shall surely be put to death.
25. The revenger of Blood shall slay the murderer.

26. The murderer shall be put to death by the mouth of two or three witnesses.
27. One witness shall not testify against any person for him to die or be convicted.
28. Thou shall put evil away from the midst of thee.
29. That prophet and that dreamer shall be put to death.
30. The prophet has spoken to turn you away from God.
31. The dreamer of dreams has spoken to turn you away from God.
32. At the mouth of two or three witness shall he be put to death.
33. Repent or the avenger of the blood will pursue the slayer.
34. The fathers shall not be put to death for the children.
35. The children shall not be put to death for the father.
36. See I have set before thee this day life and good, and death and evil.
37. I call heaven and earth to record this day against you.
38. I have set before you life and death, blessing and cursing.
39. Choose life that both thou and thy seed may live.
40. You have been rebellious against the Lord.
41. Rebellion is as the sin of witchcraft.
42. Do the greater works of the Lord.
43. Launch out into the deep.
44. Make disciples of man.
45. Become fishers of men.
46. Obey the laws of man.
47. Obey them that have rule over you.
48. Bless and not curse.
49. Do the work of the one that sent you.
50. Return to your first love.
51. Turn from your sins and receives the promises of God.
52. Love one another in all things.
53. Bear each other's burdens.
54. If you see a need meet that need, don't just pray for the need.

THE CURSES OF GOD
CURSES

1. Cursed be the man that maketh any graven or molten images.
2. Cursed for your abomination unto the Lord.
3. Cursed be the child that uncovers their parents.
4. Cursed be the child that looketh upon their parents nakedness.
5. Cursed be a child for cursing their parents.
6. Cursed be a child for cursing their elders.
7. Cursed with a curse are you for stealing God's tithe.
8. Cursed be the man that worshipped graven images.
9. Cursed be a witch and sentence to death.
10. Cursed is a man in rebellion against God.
11. Cursed is a murderer.
12. Cursed is a pervert.
13. Cursed is a thief.
14. Cursed is a deceiver of the ignorant and blind.
15. Cursed is anyone that lieth with a beast.
16. Cursed is anyone that sleepeth with his family members.
17. Cursed is he that smiteth his neighbor secretly.
18. Cursed is he that taketh bribe to kill another.
19. Cursed is he that confirmeth not the words of God's law.
20. Cursed is the soul that sinneth without repentance.
21. Cursed is a liar.
22. Cursed is a blackmailer.
23. Cursed is a manipulator and controller.
24. Cursed is a profane talker.
25. Cursed is a blasphemer.

26. Cursed is the man that walketh not in the pathway of the Lord.
27. Cursed is the man that prayeth to the dead.
28. Cursed is the man that walketh in wickedness.
29. Cursed is a jealous person.
30. Cursed is an unforgiving person.
31. Cursed is the man that stumble and fall.
32. Cursed is an hypocrite and a stumbling block.
33. Cursed is a nation that does not serve God.
34. Cursed is a people that does not worship God.
35. Cursed is an adulter and fornicator.
36. Cursed are the false teachers of the earth.
37. Cursed is the prideful and arrogant person.
38. Cursed is the one that rejects God's word.
39. Cursed is the man that rejects God's prophets.
40. Cursed is the man with the mark of the beast.
41. Cursed is the man who will not forsake all to follow Jesus.
42. Cursed is the man that loveth money.
43. Cursed is the man that setteth a trap for his enemies.
44. Cursed is a greedy person.
45. Cursed is a man that layeth a snare for his neighbors.
46. Cursed is the man that lives in misery all the days of his life.
47. Cursed is an ungrateful and unthankful person.
48. Cursed is the man that withhold from them that is in need.
49. Cursed is a covetous person.
50. Cursed is the man that liveth in darkness.
51. Cursed is the man of disobedience.
52. Cursed is the blessings of fools.
53. Cursed is the man that trusteth in riches.
54. Cursed is he that speaketh lies of God.

THE GIFT OF GOD
GIFTS

1. God has given us all good gifts.
2. God has given us eternal life.
3. God has given us the fruits of the spirit.
4. God has given us salvation freely.
5. God has given us the gift of faith.
6. God has given us the gift of love.
7. God has given us the gift of peace.
8. God has given us the gift of joy.
9. God has given us the gift of happiness.
10. God has given us the gift of healing.
11. God has given us the gift of prophecy.
12. God has given us the gift of teaching.
13. God has given us the gift of preaching.
14. God has given us the gift of evangelism.
15. God has given us the gift of apostleship.
16. God has given us the gift of dance.
17. God has given us the gift of helps.
18. God has given us the gift of ministry.
19. God has given us the gift of longsuffering.
20. God has given us the gift of wisdom.
21. God has given us the gift of knowledge.
22. God has given us the gift of understanding.
23. God has given us the gift of patience.
24. God has given us the gift of adoption.
25. God has given us the gift of sonship.
26. God has given us the gift of miracles.

27. God has given us the gift of tongues.
28. God has given us the gift of interpretation of tongues.
29. God has given us the gift of long life.
30. God has given us the gift of mercy.
31. God has given us perfect gifts.
32. God has given us heavenly gifts.
33. God has given us the gift of music.
34. God has given us the gift of giving.
35. God has given us the gift of receiving.
36. God has given us the gift of wealth.
37. God has given us the gift of prosperity.
38. God has given us the gift of fame.
39. God has given us the gift of status.
40. God has given us the gift of leadership.
41. God has given us the gift of creativity.
42. God has given us the gift of inheritance.
43. God has given us the gift of fellowship.
44. God has given us the gift of blood covenant.
45. God has given us the gift of sound mind.
46. God has given us the gift of sight.
47. God has given us the gift of mobility.
48. God has given us the gift of achievement.
49. God has given us the gift of success.
50. God has given us the gift of health
51. God has given us the gift of laughter.
52. God has given us the gift of caring.
53. God has given us the gift of signs and wonders.
54. God has given us the gift of compassion.

THUS SAYS GOD
REBUKE
Part 1

1. How long will you refuse to humble yourself before me?
2. Hear the word of the Lord.
3. I know thy rebellion, and thy stiff neck.
4. You have been rebellious against the Lord.
5. Your rebellion is witchcraft.
6. Your stubbornness in as iniquity and idolatry.
7. You have refused to obey my words.
8. You have added rebellion to your sin against me.
9. Because you are evil you rebel.
10. A cruel messenger shall be sent against you for your rebellion.
11. I will cast thee from off the face of the earth.
12. You shall die for your rebellion.
13. You have taught rebellion against the Lord.
14. Ye are of your father the devil.
15. You speak a lie and speak your own desires.
16. Let not lust reign in your mortal body.
17. Do not fulfill the lust of your flesh.
18. You cannot do the things contrary to God's will for your life.
19. Crucify the lust of your flesh.
20. Your lustful deceit will lead you into corruption.
21. Your riches have led you into temptation and a snare.
22. Flee passionate lust and follow righteousness.
23. Your lust has led you to teachers with itching ears.

24. You cannot preach me unto my people without denying yourself.
25. You must deny ungodliness and worldly lust to be mine.
26. I have not blessed you to consume it upon your lust.
27. Be my obedient child and depart from your lust and ignorance.
28. Stop yielding yourself to fleshly desires.
29. You are living in error of my word and my will for your life.
30. You are a scoffer, walking after your own lust.
31. The Lust in your eyes has betrayed you.
32. You murmur and complain while walking after your own lust.
33. You are a mocker and have walked after your own ungodly lust.
34. That which you have lusted after I have removed from thee.
35. I have taken the good and dainty from thee because of thy lust.
36. Because of your lust, that which you seek is no more.
37. Your lust shall not be satisfied.
38. I will bury you alive for your lust of the ungodly.
39. Thou shall not have whatsoever thy soul lust after.
40. I will rebuke you as I have the wind and the sea.
41. O thou of little faith, wherefore didst thou doubt God.
42. O woman, great is thy sin, Repent.
43. O faithless, why reason amongst yourselves.
44. O faithless and perverse generation, where is my word?
45. Where is your faith in unbelief?
46. Stop doubting the Most High God.
47. Woe unto you, scribes, Pharisees and hypocrites.
48. Why are you so fearful? How is it that you have no faith?
49. O faithless generation, I will consume you in my fire.
50. Be not faithless, but believing.
51. Be not weak in your faith concerning God's promises.
52. I have caused you to stumble at the stumbling stone of faith.
53. Your unbelief has caused you to be broken off from the promises of God.
54. You eat not of faith, therefore you walk by sin.

REBUKE
Part 2

1. Be not high minded but fear God.
2. Prophesy not in fear.
3. Condemn not thyself or anyone else.
4. You are a bastard of the faith and a son of devils.
5. Why call God a liar, you slothful servant.
6. You who live by fear are children of the wicked one.
7. The fruit of the spirit is not in you.
8. My word is not in your heart.
9. You are a thief and a liar; I have not spoken to you.
10. You call yourself apostle but you are not.
11. You have forsaken my laws and my words.
12. Depart from me you worker of iniquity.
13. The tempter has tempted you and your work is in vain.
14. I will not keep you from evil or withstand your enemies.
15. You will be tortured if you reject deliverance.
16. I will show no mercy to thee for thou art merciless.
17. You are blind and leading the blind.
18. You shall fall into a ditch for your ignorance.
19. Woe unto you, you blind guides.
20. You are nothing for you swear by the temple.
21. You are a blind fool swallowing camel.
22. Thou blind Pharisee, cleanse your heart first.
23. I will cause thee to sit by the high way and beg.
24. Can the blind lead the blind? You hypocrite.
25. I will cause your great multitude to be impotent and withered.

26. You are blind, how can you see the things of the spirit?
27. They which see for you shall be made blind.
28. Your sin remains in the midst of your pride.
29. Can a devil open the eyes of the blind?
30. He is not a prophet, I have not sent him.
31. I will blind your eyes and harden your hearts.
32. My chosen you will not obtain that which you seek.
33. You have become wise in your own conceit.
34. I have blinded your eyes for you cannot see.
35. Your mind has been blinded.
36. You cannot see afar off because of the sins of your past.
37. Your hatred for your brother has bound you in darkness.
38. You say you are rich and have need of nothing.
39. God has not given you power to dominate your brethren.
40. You err, not knowing the scriptures nor God's power.
41. Can devils cast out demons?
42. I will forewarn you whom you shall fear.
43. Abuse not your power in the gospel.
44. Use your power for edification and not destruction.
45. I will make an open show of your leaders.
46. Depart from me, you cursed into everlasting fire.
47. Prepare for the devil and his angels.
48. You know the law of God but yet still you are cursed.
49. You are cursed for not continuing in the faith.
50. You have been made a curse among us.
51. Curse is everyone that rejects Christ.
52. Repent and the curse will be taken away.
53. You are curse with a curse for stealing your tithe.
54. You are cursed for your rebellion against God.

REBUKE
Part 3

1. Who have you bewitched with sorceries?
2. O foolish prince, who has bewitched thee?
3. You are a witch and must not be permitted to live.
4. Why do you capture the souls of saints in your witchery?
5. You have worshipped the star of Remphan, Repent.
6. Why worship thou dead men's bones?
7. You are practicing necromancy praying to the dead.
8. You are divining for fortune and practicing black magic, stop.
9. You are prostituting the Lord's anointing.
10. You are pimping the gospel.
11. You are prostituting the gospel.
12. You are a hypocrite of deceitfulness.
13. The strong man in your house is not Jesus.
14. You practice witchcraft against my people.
15. Your days are numbers and your nights shortened.
16. The things you have seen are vain.
17. I will cast darkness upon you for your sins are great.
18. I will destroy and devour you at once.
19. I have hidden my secrets from you.
20. Touch not my anointed.
21. Touch not my prophet and do him no harm.
22. My eyes are upon you everywhere you go.
23. Nothing that you do or say is hidden from the eyes of the Lord.
24. Thou shall worship only the Lord thy God.
25. You worship me invain.

26. Why worship me in doubts?
27. You worship the star of your god Remphan.
28. You do not know what you worship.
29. You ignorantly worship the unknown god you built alters for.
30. You idolaters why worship goddess Diana and the image of Jupiter?
31. I will reveal the secrets of your hearts unto my prophets.
32. I will be worshipped and show myself as God unto all people.
33. I will break the pride of your power.
34. I know thy pride.
35. O great leader, humble yourself for the pride of your heart.
36. Your scales are your pride.
37. You looketh at all high things because of your pride.
38. God is not in all your thoughts.
39. Let not the foot of pride come against you.
40. You shall be taken and be oppressed in your pride.
41. You wear your pride like a chain around your neck.
42. Your pride shall bring you shame.
43. Your pride has caused contention in your midst.
44. In your mouth O foolish one is a rod of pride.
45. Your pride shall bring you low.
46. You are very proud and full of pride.
47. Woe unto you that wear pride as a crown upon thy head.
48. The Lord's folk are carried away captive for their pride.
49. I will bring thee down from thence saith the Lord.
50. The pride of your power shall come down.
51. Those that walk in pride will I abase.
52. You have lifted up your heart in pride and shall be rejected.
53. You have hardened your mind in pride and will lose your glory.
54. The pride of thine heart has deceived thee.

PROPHECY
HOLY—SET APART BY GOD

1. For God himself made it plain.
2. They are perceived in the things that God has made.
3. They know God.
4. The law itself is holy.
5. The commandment is holy, right and good.
6. Those whom God had chosen he set apart to be like his son.
7. Those whom God set apart, he called.
8. Everyone will confess that I am God.
9. Christ did not please himself.
10. He sent his word to all who are called to be God's holy people.
11. Wait for the Lord to reveal himself to you.
12. God will keep you firm to the very end.
13. Stay pure and be faultless until the day of Jesus Christ.
14. God is to be trusted.
15. For the place where you are standing is holy ground.
16. I have set you apart for my glory.
17. You shall be a holy man unto me.
18. You shall be a holy kingdom, a priest and an holy nation unto me.
19. Where is the holy place you have built for me to dwell?
20. Have I not given you holy garments and clothing of righteousness?
21. I have sanctified you, yet you refuse to be holy unto me.
22. Make an holy oil to anoint the temple and everything in it.
23. Why do you refuse my rebuke and continue to touch that which is not holy?

24. I made you pure and holy yet you are like a pig returning to the mud to wallow and like a dog returning to his own vomit from which he was purged.
25. Have I not clothed you in the garment of righteousness, then why do you look upon the sinful pleasures of lustful desires that destroys the soul?
26. Is this temptation greater than the power of a forgiving and merciful God?
27. When I called you, I equipped you but you doubted my abilities to deliver you from all of you sins.
28. The things of God are holy.
29. The call of God sets you apart from other.
30. You shall be holy for I am holy.
31. You defile my temple and profane my holy name, beware I will act.
32. Do not profane my holy name before the heathen.
33. Do not profane my holy name before my anointed, for they see.
34. Proclaim an holy convocation amongst the people.
35. The day is holy do not profane it.
36. Wash and be clean with holy water.
37. You are an holy people unto the Lord your God.
38. Now set your heart and your soul to seek the Lord.
39. The house of God is an holy place set aside for righteousness sake.
40. God has set him that is godly for himself.
41. God does not forget his holy promise he has made you.
42. The holy God shall sanctify you in righteousness.
43. Set your mouth against my people and prophesy my destruction.
44. You have humbled her that was set apart for pollution.
45. Turn your mouth toward the sanctuary and prophecy against it.
46. You have removed me from your heart and set up idols instead.
47. I weep for my people for they have profaned the name of God.
48. The heathens stand by and watch my people speak evil of their God.
49. The Holy Ghost is of the Lord, any other ghost is an unholy ghost.

50. My hands are outstretched to the rebellious but they refuse to return to me.
51. The more I give my children is the more they want and the further they are drawn from my presence.
52. My people have abandon me because I have given them fame, fortune and power.
53. The rituals of man has caused God to be a spectator in his temple.
54. How can a people so loved by God separate themselves from him?

THE LORD
THE LORD IS...

1. The Lord is my strength.
2. The Lord is my light.
3. The Lord is my salvation.
4. The Lord is my deliverance.
5. The Lord is my help.
6. The Lord is my strong tower.
7. The Lord is my rock.
8. The Lord is my fortress.
9. The Lord is my hiding place.
10. The Lord is my shield.
11. The Lord is my defense.
12. The Lord is my shepherd.
13. The Lord is my hope.
14. The Lord is my way out.
15. The Lord is my pathway.
16. The Lord is my resource.
17. The Lord is my shelter.
18. The Lord is my provider.
19. The Lord is my portion.
20. The Lord is my savior.
21. The Lord is my God.
22. The Lord is my king.
23. The Lord is my creator.
24. The Lord is my peace.
25. The Lord is my pavilion.

26. The Lord is my crown.
27. The Lord is my healer.
28. The Lord is my deliver.
29. The Lord is my sanctifier.
30. The Lord is my source.
31. The Lord is my joy.
32. The Lord is my protector.
33. The Lord is my defender.
34. The Lord is my guide.
35. The Lord is my keep.
36. The Lord is my judge.
37. The Lord is my redeemer.
38. The Lord is my father.
39. The Lord is my righteousness.
40. The Lord is my companion.
41. The Lord is my friend.
42. The Lord is my inheritance.
43. The Lord is my witness.
44. The Lord is my perfection.
45. The Lord is my buckler
46. The Lord is my keeper.
47. The Lord is my shade on my right hand.
48. The Lord is my encampment.
49. The Lord is my confidence.
50. The Lord is my life.
51. The Lord is my fountain of living water.
52. The Lord is my lawgiver
53. The Lord is my comfort.
54. The Lord is my helper.

EDIFICATION
BUILDING THE BODY OF CHRIST

1. I thank my God for all of you.
2. God knows that I remember you.
3. I am eager to preach the good news to you.
4. I have complete confidence in the gospel.
5. They do not give him the honor that belongs to him.
6. Surely you know that God is kind.
7. What about you?
8. You call yourself a Christian.
9. You depend on the law of Moses and boast about God.
10. For we have quoted the scripture.
11. Abraham is the spiritual father of us all.
12. I have made you father of many nations.
13. Your descendants will be as many as the stars.
14. We also boast of our troubles.
15. We know that trouble produces endurance.
16. Endurance brings Gods approval and anointing upon ones life.
17. This hope will not disappoint us.
18. Do not desire what belongs to someone else.
19. We know that the law is spiritual.
20. If God is for us, who can be against us?
21. The older will serve the younger.
22. I will take pride in my work.
23. The roots support you.

24. God does not change his mind about whom he chooses and blesses.
25. Don't think of yourself more highly than you should.
26. Be modest in your thinking.
27. Judge yourself according to the amount of faith that God gave you.
28. We have many parts in the one body.
29. Welcome those who are weak in faith.
30. Some people's faith allows them to eat anything.
31. Christ did not send me to baptize.
32. The Lord hath sworn, and will not repent; thou art a priest for ever after the order of Melchizedek.
33. As He saith also in another place, thou art a priest for ever after the order of Melchizedek.
34. Melchizedek king of Salem brings forth bread and wine: and he was the priest of the most High God.
35. And He said unto me, thou must prophesy again before many peoples, nations, tongues and kings.
36. I will be established because I am a descendant of slaves.
37. My child will be mighty upon the land because I fear the Lord.
38. Behold the former things have passed away and new things do I declare.
39. God will pour out his spirit on my child.
40. I will contend with those who contend with you and your children I will save.
41. My descendants will be known among the nations and my offspring among the peoples.
42. All who sees my children, will know that God has blessed them.
43. The children of God shall be equally yoked.
44. The men of God shall find virtuous women for mates and will not marry women with foreign gods.
45. If you do well, will you not be accepted? And if you do not do well, sin lies at the door.
46. Sin's desire is for you, but you should rule over it.

THUS SAITH THE LORD
HEART

1. I have mended your broken heart.
2. I have healed your wounded heart.
3. Set your heart to seek me.
4. I have lifted your heart.
5. I have removed your heart of stone and given you a heart of flesh.
6. I am massaging your heart.
7. I have taken away the pain from your heart.
8. I have removed the darkness from your heart.
9. I have healed your heart.
10. I have given you a new heart.
11. I have restored your heart.
12. I will make your heart fat.
13. I will turn his heart unto his son.
14. I will turn her heart unto her child.
15. I will turn your heart unto your children.
16. I will turn the hearts of the fathers unto their sons.
17. I have turned the hearts of the mothers unto their daughters.
18. Let not your heart be troubled my child.
19. I will cause your heart to rejoice.
20. I have removed the burden from your heart.
21. I have given peace unto your heart.
22. I have cleansed your heart.
23. I have fixed your heart.
24. Guard your heart from the issues of life.

25. I have strengthened your weary heart.
26. I have seen your heart and will heal you.
27. I will heal your wounded heart.
28. Guard your heart with all diligence for out of it flows the issues of life.
29. God sees that every imagination of the thoughts of your heart is evil.
30. It broke his heart.
31. It grieved him to his heart.
32. Their heart contrives evil from their infancy.
33. What have I said in my heart before God?
34. Comfort your own heart.
35. I will strengthen your heart, for the task ahead of you is great.
36. Walk in the integrity of your heart.
37. Bless me with your whole heart.
38. You have deceived my heart.
39. Try and win his heart then seek his favor.
40. When you fall in love with a maiden, win her heart and she will love you.
41. Let not your heart fail, be strong and courageous in the Lord.
42. His heart yearns for his brother.
43. His heart fainted because he did not believe.
44. When he sees you he will be glad in his heart.
45. I will harden his heart.
46. He did not lay this to heart.
47. I have harden his heart and the heart of his servants.
48. You know the heart of a stranger.
49. His heart is willing but his flesh is weak.
50. He is of a generous heart.
51. You shall not hate your brother in your heart.
52. Receive my words in your heart and hear with your ears.
53. Their uncircumcised heart is humbled.
54. Do not follow your own heart to do evil and not good.

SPIRIT

1. I have raised your spirit from the land of the dead.
2. I have given you my spirit to comfort you.
3. I have instructed my spirit to guide and to lead you.
4. I have caused my spirit to dwell within you.
5. I have seen my spirit flourishing in you.
6. I command my spirit to quicken your mortal body.
7. My spirit will reveal all truth unto you.
8. Worship me in spirit and in truth and be mines.
9. Into your hands have I committed my spirit Lord.
10. I will renew the right spirit in you.
11. There is no guile in your spirit.
12. I will heal your broken spirit.
13. My spirit will encompass you about.
14. I will cause your overwhelmed spirit to know peace.
15. I will heal your wounded spirit.
16. I will pour out my spirit upon you for a witness.
17. I will cause you to wax strong in your spirit.
18. Be born of my Holy Spirit.
19. I am with you in the spirit, the spirit of God will give you utterance.
20. Believe not every spirit my child.
21. Try the spirit by the spirit my child.
22. I have given unto you the gifts of the spirit.
23. I have called your spirit to discern spirits.
24. I command you to bear the fruits of the spirit.
25. My spirit giveth life and restoreth all things.

26. Obey the spirit of the Lord.
27. My spirit shall not always strive with man.
28. His spirit is troubled without peace and contentment.
29. I will take the spirit upon thee and place it upon them.
30. The Lord hardened his spirit.
31. Beware of the spirit of divination.
32. The spirit of God departed from him and he knew it not.
33. An evil spirit from God troubleth thee.
34. Seek not a woman with a familiar spirit.
35. Seek the counsel of God for all your concerns.
36. A double portion of my spirit will be added to you.
37. The words I speak are spirit and life.
38. He observed times, and used enchantments, and used witchcraft and dealt with a familiar spirit and with wizard.
39. The spirit of God made me and makes intercession for me.
40. The spirit lifted me up and took me away.
41. The sacrifice of God is a broken spirit.
42. My spirit made a diligent search of my heart.
43. My spirit within me is overwhelmed.
44. Put on the garment of praise for the spirit of heaviness.
45. He has an excellent spirit. Know what manner of spirit you are.
46. The spirit of whoredom is in the midst of you.
47. Cast out the unclean spirit in him.
48. Come out of the man, you unclean spirit.
49. The unclean spirit is tarring him.
50. It is a dumb and deaf spirit, cast him out.
51. Grow and wax strong in spirit, filled with wisdom and grace.
52. The spirit of the Lord is upon me because he has anointed me to preach the gospel.
53. Know what manner of spirit you are.
54. He who is born of spirit is spirit.

FIRE

1. The Lord rained upon Sodom and upon Gomorrah brimstone and fire from out of heaven.
2. Mount Sinai was altogether on smoke, because the Lord descended upon it in fire.
3. The sight of the glory of the Lord was like devouring fire on the top of the mountain.
4. It is unclean; thou shalt burn it in the fire.
5. Thou shalt not let any of thy seed pass through the fire to Molech.
6. It shall be burnt in the fire.
7. They shall be burnt with fire.
8. She shall be burnt with fire.
9. They offered strange fire before the Lord.
10. The Lord heard it and his anger was kindled; and the fire of the Lord burnt among them.
11. The fire was quenched, when Moses prayed unto the Lord.
12. And there came out from the Lord fire, and consumed the two hundred and fifty men that offered incense.
13. Scatter thou the fire yonder; for they are hallowed.
14. For there is a fire gone out of Heshbon.
15. They burnt all their cities wherein they dwelt, and all their goodly castles, with fire.
16. Glorify ye the Lord in the fires.
17. Taking the shield of faith, where with ye shall be able to quench all the fiery darts of the wicked.
18. Beloved, think it not strange concerning the fiery trial which is to try you.

19. The Lord sent fiery serpents among the people, and they bite the people and much people of Israel died.
20. Make thee a fiery serpent, and set it upon a pole that everyone that is bitten, when he looketh upon it shall live.
21. From his right hand went a fiery law for them.
22. His fruit shall be a fiery flying serpent.
23. Our God whom we serve is able to deliver us from the burning fiery furnace.
24. They were cast into the midst of the burning fiery furnace.
25. They came forth of the midst of the fire.
26. A fiery stream issued and came forth from before him.
27. His throne was like the fiery flame and his wheels as burning fire.
28. Every tree which bringeth not forth good fruit is hewn down, and cast into the fire.
29. Jesus shall baptize you with the Holy Ghost and with fire.
30. The tares are gathered and burned in the fire.
31. Jesus will burn up the chaff with unquenchable fire.
32. He shall cast them into a furnace of fire.
33. Depart from me, ye cursed, into everlasting fire prepared for the devil and his angels.
34. The fire is not quenched.
35. For every one shall be salted with fire.
36. The chaff he will burn with fire unquenchable.
37. Lord do you want us to command fire to come down from heaven and consume them.
38. I am come to send fire on the earth.
39. It rained fire and brimstone form heaven and consumed them all.
40. She beheld him as he sat by the fire.
41. There appeared unto them cloven tongues like as of fire.
42. There appeared unto him an angel of the Lord in a flame of fire in a bush.
43. He shook off the beast into the fire.
44. The fire shall try every man's work.

45. God maketh his ministers a flame of fire.
46. For our God is a consuming fire.
47. Behold, how great a matter a little fire kindleth.
48. The tongue is a fire, a world of iniquity.
49. His feet as pillars of fire.
50. His eyes were as a flame of fire.
51. These are the words of the Son of God, whose eyes are like blazing fire.
52. I counsel you to buy from me gold refined by fire, so that you may be rich.
53. Fire proceedeth out of their mouth, and devoureth their enemies.
54. He maketh fire come down from heaven on earth in the sight of men.
55. He shall be tormented with fire and brimstone in the presence of the holy angels.
56. And I saw as it were a sea of glass mingled with fire.
57. Power was given him to scorch men with fire.
58. Burn her with fire.
59. She shall be utterly burned with fire. For strong is the Lord God who judgeth her.
60. The false prophet and the beast were both cast alive into a lake of fire burning with brimstone.
61. And fire came down from God out of heaven and devoured them.
62. The devil that deceived them was cast into the lake of fire and brimstone, where the beast and false prophet are.
63. And death and hell were cast into the lake of fire.
64. And whosoever was not found written in the book of life was cast into the lake of fire.
65. The fearful, unbelieving, the abominable, murders, whoremongers, sorcerers, idolaters, and all liars, shall have their place in the lake of fire and brimstone.
66. You are a brand plucked from the fire for a great work of the Lord.
67. You were a firebrand plucked out of the burning for the purpose of God.

MARRIAGE
LET NO MAN PUT ASUNDER
Part 1

1. I will bring it forth, saith the Lord of hosts.
2. She sat over against him.
3. Isaac brought her into his mother's tent.
4. She became his wife.
5. He loved her.
6. He was comforted after his mother's death.
7. He that toucheth this man or his wife shall be put to death.
8. He called their names after the names his father had called them.
9. Now therefore forgive, I pray thee.
10. Take heed to yourselves.
11. You shall serve me.
12. She pressed him daily with her words.
13. If ought but death part thee and me.
14. It had fully been showed me.
15. Thou hast born a son.
16. Today the Lord hath brought salvation to Israel.
17. I knew it that day.
18. They were not divided.
19. They were swifter than eagles.
20. They were stronger than lions.
21. I know that I am this day king over Israel.
22. In the first days.
23. In the beginning of barley harvest.

24. He came down to meet me at Jordan.
25. The Lord hath established me.
26. The Lord hath made me a house as he promised.
27. Get thee to Anathoth, unto thine own fields.
28. Thus saith the Lord, I have healed these waters.
29. There shall not be from now anymore death or barrenness.
30. He went forth unto the spring of the waters.
31. They could not eat.
32. I have given thee fifteen years.
33. I will therefore now make preparation for it.
34. Be with him when he cometh in and when he goeth out.
35. He spoke unto him and he gave him a sign.
36. Thy breasts shall be as cluster of the vine.
37. I have not been called to come in unto the king these thirty days.
38. It cometh not.
39. Dig for it more than for hid treasures.
40. He shall redeem thee.
41. Before I go whence I shall not return.
42. He setteth an end to all my darkness.
43. He searcheth out all perfection.
44. We have heard the fame thereof with our ears.
45. Thou will bring me to the house appointed for all living.
46. Consider and hear me.
47. Lighten mine eyes.
48. Thy rod and thy staff they comfort me.
49. The upright shall have dominion over them in the morning.
50. Three days and three nights.
51. My beloved is unto me a cluster of camphor.
52. Thy stature is like a palm tree, and thy breasts to clusters of grapes.
53. I will go up to the palm tree; I will take hold of the boughs thereof.
54. My soul desired the first ripe fruit.

LET NO MAN PUT ASUNDER
Part 2

1. The new wine is found in the cluster.
2. A blessing is in it.
3. He shall not approach.
4. Thou shall not be respecter of persons.
5. Behold, here I am.
6. I will restore it to you.
7. Thou shall not come in here.
8. He shall be chief and captain.
9. The Lord raiseth me.
10. Thy love, loveth me.
11. I will bring them by a way they know not.
12. I will lead them in paths they have not known.
13. He giveth goodly word.
14. I have pronounced him clean.
15. The spirit of the Lord came mightily upon him.
16. I have loosed him.
17. I will let him go free and cause him to find you.
18. The Lord hast loosed my bonds.
19. I am thy servant and the son of thine handmaid.
20. I have loosed the captive mind.
21. I have loosed the silver cord that bound him.
22. I have broken the golden bowl that held him prisoner.
23. I have broken the pitcher at the fountain for your sake.
24. I have broken the wheel at the cistern that burdens him down.
25. He shall never be weary or stumble again.

26. Go and loose the sackcloth from off thy loin for I have wrought deliverance.
27. Thy tacklings are loosed and he is free.
28. They could not spread the sail to send him drifting any longer.
29. I have divided the spoiled and you shall receive your portion.
30. Keep your gates open to receive the visitors.
31. Arise and shake thy self for the battle has began.
32. I have chosen this fast to loose the bands of wickedness.
33. Behold I have loose thee this day from the chains upon thy hands.
34. If it seem good unto thee come with me, come.
35. I will look well unto thee if thou come with me.
36. You are walking in the midst of the fire.
37. That which was made to destroy you have not hurt you.
38. Thou hast given into my hands a great deliverance.
39. He is a mighty man of valor.
40. They set themselves in the midst of the parcel and delivered it.
41. They have humbled themselves and I have forgiven them.
42. Hold your peace at this time.
43. Thou art my hiding place.
44. Thou shall preserve me from trouble.
45. Thou shall compass me about with songs of deliverance.
46. We have been with child.
47. We have been in pain.
48. The house of Jacob shall posses their possession.
49. He shall even restore the principal.
50. He that is perfect in knowledge is with thee.
51. A faithful witness will not lie.
52. A just weight is his delight.
53. I esteem all thy precepts concerning all things to be right.
54. Through thy precepts I get understanding.

THE RIGHTS OF PASSAGE
Part 3

1. I ask that God will make it possible for me to visit you now.
2. For I want very much to see you.
3. Many times, I have planned to visit you.
4. Something has always kept me from visiting you.
5. We wait for it with patience.
6. I promised you a mate of your hearts desire.
7. At the right time.
8. I will come back.
9. I love Jacob.
10. I will have mercy on anyone I wish.
11. I will take pity on anyone I wish.
12. One for special occasions and the other for ordinary use.
13. I will call my beloved.
14. Love must be completely sincere.
15. Love one another warmly as Christian.
16. Let your hope keep you joyful.
17. Be patient in troubles, and pray at all times.
18. Be happy with those who are happy.
19. Weep with those who weep.
20. Have the same concern for everyone.
21. Do not be proud but accept humble duties.
22. Do not think of yourselves as wise.
23. The only obligation you have is to love one another.
24. Do not desire what belongs to someone else.
25. Love your neighbor as you love yourself.

26. If you love others, you will never do them wrong.
27. To love is to obey the law.
28. The night is nearly over, day is almost here.
29. Let us conduct ourselves properly.
30. We should not please ourselves.
31. Accept one another.
32. The decision was their own.
33. When I come to you, I will bless you with all.
34. I know that I shall come with a full measure of Christ blessings.
35. I will come to you full of joy.
36. I am grateful to them.
37. I am happy about you.
38. Everyone has heard of your loyalty to the gospel.
39. God will soon crush Satan under your feet.
40. May God our father and the Lord Jesus Christ give you grace and peace.
41. I always give thanks to my God for you.
42. For in union with Christ you have become rich in all things.
43. The message about Christ has become so firmly established in you.
44. You have not failed to receive a single blessing.
45. I appeal to you to agree in what you say.
46. Let there be no division between you.
47. Be completely united with only one thought and one purpose.
48. I have heard that there are quarrels among you.
49. Each one of you say something different.
50. Strengthen the weaker vessel.
51. Show compassion, good and benevolence at all times.
52. There is strength in unity.
53. Despise not the wife of your youth.
54. Cherish the gifts of God unto yourself with great joy.

ENEMY
MY ENEMIES ARE MY FRIENDS

1. I love my enemies.
2. I pray blessings upon my enemies.
3. I show my enemies mercy.
4. I show my enemies favor.
5. I give of my time in prayer for my enemy's deliverance.
6. My enemies are pushing me into my destiny with God.
7. My enemies give God reasons to make a way for me.
8. My enemies make ways out of no way for me.
9. My enemies bless me when they try to curse me.
10. God turned my enemies curse into a blessing for me.
11. My enemies keep me on my knees in prayer to God.
12. My enemies cause the anointing to increase upon my life.
13. My enemies are good for business.
14. My enemies cause me to watch, fast and pray continually.
15. My enemies cause me to seek God's face daily.
16. My enemies affirm my faithfulness to God.
17. My enemies are possessed by demonic spirits and powers.
18. I forgive my enemies and God forgives me.
19. I intercede for my enemies and God blesses me abundantly.
20. I seek peace with my enemies at all time.
21. God made my enemies to be at peace with me.
22. My enemies are my footstool and ladder of elevation.
23. I make enemies when I do the will of my father in heaven.
24. My enemies fuel me up with desires to pray all night.
25. My enemies perfect the work of God in me.

26. Life without enemies is none productive.
27. My enemies expose my imperfections.
28. My enemies cause me to be strong and resilient.
29. My enemies favors me.
30. My enemies bless me with opportunities to excel.
31. My enemies destroy the traces of Satan within me.
32. My enemies keep me on my knees.
33. My enemies keep me active with God.
34. My enemies lead me to witty ideas and new inventions.
35. My enemies are working for God and me.
36. My enemies are fulfilling God's prophecy for my life.
37. My enemies are my catalyst for greatness in God.
38. My enemy's eyes are focused on me.
39. I sparkle like diamond in the sight of my enemies.
40. My enemies are afraid of me.
41. My enemies are cowards hiding behind walls.
42. My enemies have taken their eyes off Jesus and placed them on me.
43. I am the center of attraction for my enemies.
44. God fights with my enemies in battle.
45. God pursues and overtake my enemies.
46. God defends me from my enemies.
47. God answers my enemies by fire.
48. God contends with my enemies on my behalf.
49. God makes war with my enemies.
50. God leads my enemies astray to destruction.
51. My enemies have been anointed to push me into greatness.
52. I need my enemies to keep pushing me forward.

SIN
WHAT IS SIN?
Part 1

1. They say they are wise, but they are fools.
2. They do shameful things with each other.
3. They exchange the truth about God for a lie.
4. They worship and serve what God has created.
5. God has given them over to shameful passions.
6. He has given them over to corrupted minds.
7. They do the things that they should not do.
8. They are filled with all kinds of wickedness, evil and greed.
9. They are full of jealousy, murder, fighting, deceit and malice.
10. They gossip and speak evil of one another.
11. They are hateful to God, insolent, proud and boastful.
12. They think of more ways to do evil.
13. They disobey their parents. ·
14. They have no conscience.
15. They do not keep their promises.
16. They show no kindness or pity for others.
17. You have no excuse at all.
18. Do you, my friend pass judgment on others?
19. You condemn yourself.
20. Do you think you will escape God's judgment?
21. Other people are selfish and reject what is right.
22. God will pour out his anger and fury.
23. For God judge everyone by the same standard.

24. They sin and are lost apart from the law.
25. They sin and are judged by the law.
26. They deny doing what the law says.
27. Their conscience also show that this is true.
28. Their thoughts sometimes accuse them and sometimes defend them.
29. God will judge the secret thoughts of all.
30. Because of Christians, the sinners speak evil of God.
31. Christians will be condemned by sinners because they break the law.
32. All human beings are liars.
33. All have turned away from God.
34. They have all gone wrong.
35. They leave ruin and destruction wherever they go.
36. They have not known the path of peace.
37. They have not learned reverence for God.
38. Sin not in God's sight.
39. Where sin increased, God's grace increased much more.
40. For sin pays its wage of death.
41. Sin is a dead thing.
42. Sin sprang to life, and I died.
43. Sin brought death to me.
44. I am mortal, sold as a slave to sin.
45. I do what I hate.
46. I don't do what I would like to do.
47. I am not able to do it.
48. I don't do the good I want to do.
49. I do the evil that I do not want to do.
50. It is the sin that lives in me.
51. To be controlled by human nature results in death.
52. They do not obey God's law, they cannot obey it.
53. You are going to die.
54. For creation was condemned.

WHAT IS SIN?
Part 2

1. For your sake we are in danger of death at all times.
2. We are treated like sheep that are going to be killed.
3. God makes stubborn anyone he wishes.
4. Who can resist God's will?
5. Who are you, my friend, to talk back to God?
6. You are not my people living in sin and iniquity.
7. They have tried to set up their own way.
8. They did not submit themselves to God's way.
9. It is true that they did not hear the message.
10. They are trying to kill me.
11. I am speaking now to you sinners.
12. How can you be proud?
13. They were broken off because they did not believe.
14. He is severe toward those who have fallen.
15. Anything that is not based on faith is sin.
16. Keep away from them.
17. By their fine words and flattering speech they deceived many.
18. I defeat sin and evil pleasure by trusting in Christ to help me at all times.
19. Every wrong is a sin.
20. Sin lies at the door.
21. Thou art brought on me and my kingdom a great sin.
22. What is my trespass? What is my sin?
23. How can I do this great wickedness and sin against God?
24. Do not sin against the child.

25. It is a sin offering.
26. You have sinned a great sin.
27. I shall make an atonement for your sin.
28. In the day when I visit I will visit their sin upon them.
29. God forgives iniquity, transgression and sin.
30. The iniquities of the father's visit the children's children up to four generations.
31. God will pardon our iniquity and sin.
32. If the priest that is anointed does sin let him bring an unblemished sin offering.
33. Rebuke anyone who sins or you will be equally guilty.
34. The sin which he hath done shall be for given him.
35. They shall bear their sin.
36. Anyone who curses God shall bear his sin.
37. That man shall bear his sin.
38. Shall one person sin and you become angry with the whole congregation?
39. It is a purification for sin.
40. He died in his own sin.
41. Should you sin against the Lord your God?
42. There is in the woman no sin worthy of death.
43. If you forbear to vow, it shall not be a sin to thee.
44. Every man shall be put to death for his own sin.
45. God forbid that I should sin against the Lord in ceasing to pray for you.
46. For rebellion is as the sin of witchcraft.
47. I pray thee pardon my sin.
48. Will you sin against innocent blood?
49. Let not the king sin against his servant.
50. What is my sin before thy father that he seeks my life?
51. And this thing became a sin.
52. The trespass money and sin money was not brought into the house of the Lord.
53. Cover not their iniquity and let not their sin be blotted out from before thee.
54. Even Solomon did outlandish woman cause to sin.

WHAT IS SIN?
Part 3

1. In all this, Job did not sin with his lips.
2. If I sin, then thou markest me, and thou will not acquit me from mine iniquity.
3. How many are mine iniquities & sins? Make me to know my transgression & my sin.
4. His bones are full of the sin of his youth.
5. I have not suffered my mouth to sin by wishing a curse to his soul.
6. What profit shall I have if I be cleansed from my sin?
7. In your anger do not sin.
8. Blessed is he whose transgression is forgiven, whose sin is covered.
9. I acknowledge my sin unto thee, and mine iniquity have I not hid.
10. There is no rest in my bones because of my sin.
11. I will declare my iniquity and I will be sorry for my sin.
12. I will take heed to my ways that I sin not with my tongue.
13. Wash me thoroughly from mine iniquity, and cleanse me form my sin.
14. Behold, I was shaped in iniquity, and in sin did my mother conceive me.
15. For the sin of their mouth and the words of their lips let them be taken in their pride.
16. The labor of the righteous tends to life, but the fruit of the wicked tends to sin.

17. When words are many, sin is not absent.
18. Sin is a reproach to any people.
19. Who can say, I have made my heart clean, I am pure from my sin?
20. A high look, and a proud heart, and the plowing of the wicked is sin.
21. The thought of foolishness is sin.
22. Suffer not thy mouth to cause thy flesh to sin, and destroy the work of thine hand.
23. He bared the sin of many, and made intercession for the transgressors.
24. I will recompense their iniquity and their sin double.
25. They eat up the sin of my people, and thy set their heart on their iniquity.
26. His sin is hid.
27. She is the beginning of the sin to the daughter of Zion.
28. All manner of sin and blasphemy shall be forgiven unto men.
29. Behold the Lamb of God, which taketh away the sin of the world.
30. Behold, thou art made whole sin no more, lest a worse thing come unto thee.
31. He that is without sin among you let him first cast a stone at her.
32. I do not condemn thee, go and sin no more.
33. Whosoever committeth sin is the servant of sin.
34. But now they have no cloak for their sin.
35. He will reprove the world of sin, righteousness and judgment.
36. Lay not this sin to their charge.
37. They are all under sin.
38. By the Law is the knowledge of sin.
39. Blessed is the man whom sin the Lord will not count against him.
40. Sin entered the world by one man which leads to death for all have sinned.
41. For he that is dead is freed from sin.
42. Let not sin reign in your mortal body.
43. For sin shall not have dominion over you.

44. For we know that the law is spiritual: but I am carnal, sold to sin.
45. Awake to righteousness, and sin not; some have not the knowledge of God.
46. The sting of death is sin, and the strength of sin is the law.
47. When lust has conceived; it bringeth forth sin.
48. But if you have respect to persons, ye commit sin.
49. To him that knows to do good, and does it not, to him it is sin.
50. If we say we have no sin, we deceive ourselves.
51. He that commits sin transgresses the law: for sin is the transgression of the law.
52. Whosoever is born of God doth not commit sin.
53. He cannot sin, because he is born of God
54. All unrighteousness is sin.

JUDGMENT
THE WAGES OF SIN IS DEATH
Part 1

1. Will you plead for Baal?
2. If he be a god, let him plead for himself.
3. Cast them down to the ground.
4. He cursed the Lord's anointed
5. Should this day be adversaries unto me?
6. They fell, all seven together.
7. The sorrows of hell compass me all about.
8. The snares of death prevented me.
9. He cursed me with a grievous curse.
10. O thou man of God, there is death in the pot.
11. Every man shall be put to death for his own sin.
12. The Lord smote the king.
13. Set thine house in order; for thou shall die, and not live.
14. He did evil in the sight of the Lord.
15. They were his counselors after his father's death to his destruction.
16. He was cut off from the house of the Lord.
17. Let judgment be executed speedily upon him.
18. Let darkness and the shadow of death stain it.
19. Let the blackness of the day terrify it.
20. My soul chooseth strangling.
21. A land of darkness.
22. Without any order, the light is as darkness.
23. He discovered deep things out of darkness.

24. My face is foul with weeping.
25. It shall devour the strength of his skin.
26. His widows shall not weep.
27. There is no darkness where the workers of iniquity may hide themselves.
28. Have the gates of death been open unto thee?
29. Have thou seen the doors of the shadow of death?
30. In death there is no remembrance of thee.
31. In the grave who shall give thee thanks?
32. He ordaineth his arrows against the persecutors.
33. Consider my trouble which I suffer of them that hate me.
34. My strength is dried up like a potsherd.
35. My tongue cleaveth to my jaws.
36. Thou hast sore broken us in the place of dragons.
37. Thou hast brought me into the dust of death.
38. Their beauty shall consume in the grave from their dwelling.
39. They tempted God in their heart.
40. They were not estranged from their lust.
41. I gave them up unto their own hearts lust: and they walked in their own counsels.
42. They lusted exceedingly in the wilderness, and tempted God in the desert.
43. Woe is me! For I am as when thy have gathered the summer fruits.
44. The gift blindeth the wise and perverteth the words of the righteous.
45. Cursed be he that maketh the blind to wander out of the way.
46. The Lord shall smite thee with madness.
47. Thou shalt not prosper in thy ways.
48. Thou shalt be only oppressed and spoiled evermore.
49. No man shall save thee.
50. Smite this people, I pray thee with blindness.
51. He smote them with blindness.
52. The blind and the lame shall not come into the house.
53. We stumble at noonday as in the night.
54. We are in desolate places as dead men.

THE WAGES OF SIN IS DEATH
Part 2

1. Hear, ye deaf: and look, ye blind, that ye may see.
2. Who is blind, but my servant.
3. Who is deaf as my messenger that I sent?
4. Who is blind as he that is perfect, and blind as the Lord's servant?
5. His watchmen are blind.
6. They are all ignorant.
7. They are all dumb dogs, they cannot bark, sleeping, lying down to sleep.
8. They have polluted themselves with blood.
9. I will bring distress upon men.
10. They shall walk like blind men.
11. They have sinned against the Lord.
12. I will strike every horse with astonishment and every rider with madness.
13. Will he be please with thee?
14. Loose his shoe from off his foot, and spit in his face.
15. Even that it would please God to destroy me.
16. He would let loose his hand and cut me off!
17. He hath loosed my cord, and afflicted me.
18. O captive daughter of Zion.
19. His thoughts troubled him.
20. Our God hast punished us less than our iniquity deserves.
21. We have not wrought any deliverance in the earth.
22. Thou shall not bear false witness against thy neighbor.
23. Thou shall not raise a false report.

24. I will not justify the wicked.
25. You shall not steal, neither deal falsely, neither lie one to another.
26. You shall not swear by my name falsely.
27. You shall not profane the name of thy God, I am the Lord.
28. There is no matter hid from the king.
29. How then comfort ye me invain?
30. In your answers there remaineth falsehood.
31. Behold he travaileth with iniquity and hath conceived mischief.
32. Deliver me not over unto the will of mine enemies.
33. I hate every false way.
34. Thou hast trodden down all them that err from thy statutes.
35. Whose mouth speaketh vanity?
36. Rid me, and deliver me from the hand of strange children.
37. A false witness shall not be unpunished.
38. He that speaketh lies shall perish.
39. He that speaketh lies shall not escape.
40. We have made lies our refuge.
41. Under falsehood have we hid ourselves.
42. The prophets prophesy falsely.
43. The priest bear rule by their means.
44. My people love to have it so.
45. Every man is brutish in his knowledge.
46. The prophets prophesy lies in my name, I sent them not.
47. They prophesy unto you false vision and divination.
48. Behold, I am against them that prophesy false dreams.
49. They shall not profit this people at all.
50. It is false.
51. Thou shall not do this thing.
52. The prophets have seen vain and foolish things for thee.
53. They have not discovered thine iniquity.
54. He will call to remembrance their iniquity.

THE WAGES OF SIN IS DEATH
Part 3

1.   Let none of you imagine evil in your hearts against his neighbor.
2.   For the idols have spoken vanity.
3.   The diviners have seen a lie.
4.   They were troubled, because there was no shepherd.
5.   I will come near to you to judgment.
6.   I will be a swift witness against the sorcerers.
7.   Let me not see the death of the child.
8.   She lifted up her voice and wept.
9.   I know not the day of my death.
10.   Whosoever toucheth the mount shall be put to death.
11.   It is a crime to hit your parents.
12.   It is a sin to curse your parents.
13.   They offered before the Lord and died.
14.   Their blood shall be upon them.
15.   A man or woman with familiar spirit shall be put to death.
16.   A wizard shall be put to death.
17.   The Lord hath not sent me.
18.   I have given unto you the priest's office as a service of gift.
19.   Let me die the death of the righteous.
20.   Thou shall put evil away from the midst of thee.
21.   The bitterness of death has past.
22.   There is but a step between me and death.
23.   He cast them down to the ground.
24.   The floods of ungodly men made me afraid.
25.   I will not put thee to death by the sword.

26. He was cut off from the house of the Lord.
27. The judges shall make diligent inquisition.
28. Behold, he travaileth with iniquity, and hath conceived mischief.
29. Those who practice magic shall be cast into the fire.
30. For I know that after my death ye will utterly corrupt yourself.
31. Evil will befall you in the latter days.
32. You will turn aside from the way which I have commanded you.
33. Because of your nature you will do evil in the sight of the Lord.
34. You have provoked the Lord to anger through the work of your hands.
35. By her teachings, she misleads my servants.
36. You are a liar both in words and in deeds.
37. Their words are full of deadly deceit.
38. Their speech is filled with bitter curses.
39. They are quick to hurt and kill.
40. God made their minds and hearts dull.
41. I will take revenge, I will pay back, says the Lord.
42. Let us stop judging one another.

SCRIPTURES FOR PASTORS

1. Now therefore go, and I will be with thy mouth, and teach thee what thou shalt say. (Ex. 4:12)
2. I will be with thy mouth, and with his mouth, and will teach you what ye shall do. (Ex. 4:15)
3. Thou shalt teach them ordinances and laws, and shalt show them the way wherein they must walk, and the work that they must do. (Ex. 18:20)
4. He hath put in his heart that he may teach. (Ex. 35:34)
5. The Lord commanded me at that time to teach you statues and judgments. (Deu. 4:14)
6. Thou shalt teach them diligently unto thy children. (Deu. 6:7)
7. Do according to all that the priests the Levites shall teach you. (Deu. 24:8)
8. And thou hast also appointed prophets to preach of thee at Jerusalem. (Neh. 6:7)
9. Teach me, and I will hold my tongue: and cause me to understand wherein I have erred. (Job 6:24)
10. Shall not they teach thee, and tell thee, and utter words out of their heart. (Job 8:10)
11. They shall teach thee. (Job 12:7)
12. It shall teach thee. (Job 12:8)
13. Shall any teach God knowledge? (Job 21:22)
14. I will teach you by the hand of God: that which is with the almighty will I not conceal. (Job 27:11)
15. Days should speak, and multitude of years should teach wisdom. (Job 32:7)

16. Hearken unto me: hold thy peace, and I shall teach thee wisdom. (Job 33:33)
17. That which I see not teach thou me: if I have done iniquity, I will do no more. (Job 34:32)
18. Teach us what we shall say unto him; for we cannot order our speech by reason of darkness. (Job 37:19)
19. Show me thy ways, O Lord; teach me thy paths. (Ps. 25:4)
20. Teach me: for thou art the God of my salvation. (Ps. 25:5)
21. Good and upright is the Lord: therefore will he teach sinners in the way. (Ps. 25:8)
22. The meek will he teach his way. (Ps. 25:9)
23. What man is he that feareth the Lord? Him shall he teach in the way that he shall choose. (Ps. 25:12)
24. Teach me thy way, O Lord and lead me in a plain path, because of mine enemies. (Ps. 27:11)
25. I will instruct thee and teach thee in the way which thou shalt go. (Ps. 32:8)
26. I will teach you the fear of the Lord. (Ps. 34:11)
27. Thy right hand shall teach thee terrible things. (Ps. 45:4)
28. Then will I teach transgressors thy ways: and sinners shall be converted unto thee. (Ps. 51:13)
29. Teach me thy way, O Lord; I will walk in thy truth: unite my heart to fear they name. (Ps. 86:11)
30. Teach his senators wisdom. (Ps. 105:22)
31. Teach me good judgment and knowledge. (Ps. 119:66)
32. Teach me to do thy will; for thou art my God: thy spirit is good. (Ps. 143:10)
33. Teach a just man, and he will increase in learning. (Prov. 9:9)
34. He will teach us of his ways, and we will walk in his paths. (Isa. 2:3)
35. Whom shall he teach knowledge? And whom shall he make to understand doctrine? Them that are weaned from the milk, and drawn from the breasts. (Isa. 28:9)
36. For his God doth instruct him to discretion, and doth teach him. (Isa. 28:26)

37. The spirit of the Lord God is upon me; because the Lord hath anointed me to preach good tidings unto the meek. (Isa. 61:1)
38. Hear the word of the Lord, O ye women, and let your ear receive the word of his mouth, and teach your daughters wailing. (Jer. 9:20)
39. They shall teach my people the difference between the holy and profane, and cause them to discern between the unclean and the clean. (Ezek. 44:23)
40. Arise, go unto Nineveh, that great city, and preach unto it the preaching that I bid thee. (Jonah 3:2)
41. Jesus began to preach, and to say, Repent: for the kingdom of heaven is at hand. (Matt. 4:17)
42. And as ye go, preach, saying, the kingdom of heaven is at hand. (Matt. 10:7)
43. The poor have the gospel preached to them. (Matt. 11:5)
44. This gospel of the kingdom shall be preached in all the world for a witness unto all nations. (Matt. 24:14)
45. He departed thence to teach and to preach in their cities. (Matt.11:1)
46. Preach the baptism of repentance for the remission of sins. (Mk. 1:4)
47. Preached, saying, There cometh one mightier than I after me. (Mk. 1:7)
48. Let us go into the next towns that I may preach there also. (Mk. 1:38)
49. He preached in their synagogues throughout all Galilee, and cast out devils. (Mk. 1:39)
50. He preached the word unto them. (Mk. 2:2)
51. They went out, and preached that men should repent. (Mk. 6:12)
52. Wheresoever this gospel shall be preached throughout the whole world. (Mk. 14:9)
53. Go ye into all the world, and preach the gospel to every creature. (Mk. 16:15)
54. They went forth, and preached every where, the Lord working with them, and confirming the word with signs following. (Mk. 16:20)

55. Many other things in his exhortation preached he unto the people. (Lk. 3:18)
56. The spirit of the Lord is upon me, because he hath anointed me to preach the gospel to the poor; he hath sent me to heal the brokenhearted, to preach deliverance to the captives, and recovering of sight to the blind, to set at liberty them that are bruised. (Lk. 4:18)
57. To preach the acceptable year of the Lord. (Lk. 4:19)
58. I must preach the kingdom of God to other cities also: for therefore am I sent. (Lk. 4:43)
59. He preached in the synagogues of Galilee. (Lk. 4:44)
60. He sent them to preach the kingdom of God, and to heal the sick. (Lk. 9:2)
61. Let the dead bury the dead: but go thou and preach the kingdom of God. (Lk. 9:60)
62. Since that time the kingdom of God is preached, and every man presseth into it. (Lk. 16:16)
63. And that repentance and remission of sins should be preached in his name among all nations. (Lk. 24:47)
64. They taught the people, and preached through Jesus the resurrection from the dead. (Acts 4:2)
65. When they believed Philip preaching the things concerning the kingdom of God, and the name of Jesus Christ, they were baptized, both men and women. (Acts 8:12)
66. Then Philip opened his mouth, and began at the same scripture, and preached unto him Jesus. (Acts 8:35)
67. Passing through he preached in all the cities. (Acts 8:40)
68. And straightway he preached Christ in the synagogues, that he is the Son of God. (Acts 9:20)
69. He commanded us to preach unto the people, and to testify that it is he which was ordained of God to be the Judge of quick and dead. (Acts. 10:42)
70. When they were at Salamis, they preached the word of God in the synagogues of the Jews. Acts 13:5

71. We also are men of like passions with you, and preach unto you that ye should turn from these vanities unto the living God. (Acts 14:15)
72. Let us go again and visit our brethren in every city where we have preached the word of the Lord. (Acts 5:36)
73. They were forbidden of the Holy Ghost to preach the word in Asia. (Acts 16:6)
74. Paul preached unto them. (Acts 20:7)
75. I am ready to preach the gospel to you that are at Rome also. (Rom. 1:15)
76. The word is nigh thee, even in thy mouth, and in thy heart: that is, the word of faith, which we preach. (Rom. 10:8)
77. How shall they believe in him of whom they have not heard? And how shall they hear without a preacher? (Rom. 10:14)
78. How shall they preach, except they be sent? (Rom. 10:15)
79. I have fully preached the gospel of Christ. (Rom. 15:19)
80. So Have I strived to preach the gospel. (Rom. 15:20)
81. For Christ sent me not to baptize, but to preach the gospel. (1 Cor. 1:17)
82. Even so hath the Lord ordained that they which preach the gospel should live of the gospel. (1 Cor. 1:14)
83. For though I preach the gospel, I have nothing to glory of: for necessity is laid upon me; yea, woe is unto me, if I preach not the gospel. (1 Cor. 9:16)
84. When I peach the gospel, I may make the gospel of Christ without charge, that I abuse not my power in the gospel. (1 Cor. 9:18)
85. I declare unto you the gospel which I preached unto you, which also ye have received, and wherein ye stand. (1 Cor. 15:1)
86. If you keep in memory what I preached unto you. (1 Cor. 15:2)
87. Therefore whether it were I or they, so we preach, and so ye believed. (1Cor. 15:11)
88. Now if Christ be preached that he rose from the dead, how say some among you that there is no resurrection of the dead. (1 Cor. 15:12)
89. For we preach not ourselves, but Christ the Lord. (2 Cor. 4:5)

90. To preach the gospel in the regions beyond you, and not to boast in another man's line of things made ready to our hand. (2 Cor. 10:16)
91. If any man preach any other gospel unto you that ye have received, let him be accursed. (Gal. 1:9)
92. That I might preach him among the heathen. (Gal. 1:16)
93. I went up by revelation, and communicated unto them that gospel which I preach among the Gentiles. (Gal. 2:2)
94. Ye know how through infirmity of the flesh I preached the gospel unto you at the first. (Gal. 4:13)
95. And came and preached peach to you which were afar off and to them that were nigh. (Eph. 2:17)
96. I should preach among the Gentiles the unsearchable riches of Christ. (Eph. 3:8)
97. Whom we preach, warning every man, and teaching every man in all wisdom; that we may present every man perfect in Christ Jesus. (Col. 1:28)
98. Preach the word; be instant in season, out of season; reprove, rebuke, exhort with all long suffering and doctrine. (2 Tim.4:2)
99. For this cause was the gospel preached also to them that are dead, that thy might be judged according to men in the flesh, but live according to God in the spirit. (1 Pet. 4:6)
100. They to whom it was first preached entered not in because of unbelief. (Heb. 4:6)

SCRIPTURES FOR PROPHETS

1. I perceived that God had not sent him, but he pronounced this prophecy against me. (Neh. 6:12)
2. And though I have the gift of prophecy, and understand all mysteries, I am nothing. (1 Cor. 13:2)
3. Neglect not the gift that is in thee, which was given thee by prophecy. (1 Tim. 4:14)
4. No prophecy of the scripture is of any private interpretation. (2 Pet. 1:20)
5. When the spirit rested upon them, they prophesied, and did not cease. (Num. 11:25)
6. I hate him: for he never prophesied good unto me, but always evil. (2 Chron. 18:7)
7. Believe the Lord your God, and be established; believe his prophets, so shall ye prosper. (2 Chron. 20:20)
8. Touch not mine anointed, and do my prophets no harm. (1 Chron. 16:22 / Ps. 105:15)
9. I have not sent these prophets, I have not spoken to them, yet they prophesied. (Jer. 23:21)
10. They spake of Jerimiah, this man is worthy to die, for he hath prophesied against this city. (Jer. 26:11)
11. The Lord sent me to prophecy against this house & this city all the words that ye have heard. (Jer. 26:12)
12. Amend your ways and doings, obey the voice of the Lord your God spoken by the prophet. (Jer. 26:13)
13. The prophets prophecy falsely, and the priests bear rule by their means, my people love it so. (Jer. 5:31)

14. They prophecy unto you a false vision and divination, and the deceit of their heart. (Jer. 14:14)
15. By sword and famine shall the false prophets prophesying in my name be consumed. (Jer. 14:15)
16. Hearken not unto the words of the prophets that prophesy unto you, they make you vain. (Jer. 23:16)
17. Behold, I am against them that prophesy false dreams and cause my people to err by lies. (Jer. 23:32)
18. Behold, I am against the prophets, that use their tongues, and say He (I) saith. (Jer. 23:31)
19. Both prophets and priest are profane: yea in my house have I found their wickedness. (Jer. 23:11)
20. The prophet that hath a dream let him tell it, and my words, let him speak it faithfully.(Jer. 23:28)
21. Everyone is covetous, from the prophet even unto the priest everyone dealeth falsely. (Jer. 6:13)
22. Before I formed thee in the belly I knew thee; I ordained thee a prophet unto the nations. (Jer. 1:5)
23. The priest and the prophet have erred through strong drink; they are swallowed up of wine. (Isa. 28:7)
24. Prophesy not unto us right things, speak unto us smooth things, prophesy deceits. (Isa. 30:10)
25. Many will say unto me Lord, Lord, have we not prophesied in thy name and cast out devils. (Mt. 7:22)
26. He that receiveth a prophet in the name of a prophet shall receive a prophet's reward. (Mt. 10:41)
27. A prophet is not without honour, save in his own country, and in his own house. (Mt. 13:57)
28. For greater is he that prophesieth than he that speaketh with tongues, except he interprets. (1 Cor.14:5)
29. He that prophesieth speaketh unto men to edification, and exhortation, and comfort. (1 Cor. 14:3)
30. He that speaketh unknown tongue edifieth self; but he that prophesieth edifieth the church. (1 Cor. 14:4)
31. And the spirits of the prophets are subject to the prophets. (1 Cor. 14:32)

32. For we know in part, and we prophesy in part. (1 Cor. 13:9)
33. If the prophet be deceived when he hath spoken a thing, I the Lord have deceived that prophet. (Ezek. 14:9)
34. When this cometh to pass, then shall they know that a prophet hath been among them. (Ezek. 33:33)
35. Prophesy against the shepherds of Israel, woe to the shepherds of Israel that feed themselves. (Ezek. 34:2)
36. Prophesy unto the mountains of Israel, say, Ye mountains of Israel, hear the word of the Lord. (Ezek. 36:1)
37. Prophesy unto the wind, come from the four winds, O breath, and breathe upon the slain. (Ezek. 37:9)
38. Prophesy, O my people, I will open your graves, & cause you to come up out of your graves. (Ezek. 37:12)
39. I will pour out my spirit upon all flesh, your sons & your daughters shall prophecy. (Joel 2:28 / Acts 2:17)
40. The lion hath roared, who will not fear? The Lord God hath spoken, who can but prophesy? (Amos 3:8)
41. The Lord God will do nothing, but he revealeth his secret unto his servants the prophets. (Amos 3:7)
42. The prophets divine for money: yet will they lean upon the Lord, & say the Lord is with us. (Micah 3:11)
43. Shall the priest and the prophet be slain in the sanctuary of the Lord? (Lam. 2:20)
44. The same man had four daughters, virgins, which did prophesy. (Acts. 21:9)
45. A prophet shall the Lord your God raise up unto you of your brethren. (Acts 3:22 / Deu. 18:15)
46. Let us prophesy according to the proportion of faith. (Rom. 12:6)
47. Now restore the man his wife; for he is a prophet, and he shall pray for you and you shall live. (Gen. 20:7)
48. Thou must prophesy again before many peoples, and nations, and tongues, and kings. (Rev. 10:11)
49. Despise not prophesying. (1 Thess. 5:20)
50. Whosoever will not hearken unto my words spoken by my prophets, I will require it of him. (Deu. 18:19)

51. When a prophet speak in my name & it does not come to pass, fear not, he speaks his heart. (Deu. 18:22)
52. The woman saith unto him, Sir, I perceive that thou art a prophet. (Jhn. 47:19)

SCRIPTURES FOR TEACHERS

1. Now therefore go, and I will be with thy mouth, and teach thee what thou shalt say. (Ex. 4:12)
2. I will be with thy mouth, and with his mouth, and will teach you what ye shall do. (Ex. 4:15)
3. Thou shalt teach them ordinances and laws, and shalt show them the way wherein they must walk, and the work that they must do. (Ex. 18:20)
4. That thou mayest teach them. (Ex. 24:12)
5. He hath put in his heart that he may teach. (Ex. 35:34)
6. That ye may teach the children of Israel all the statues which the Lord hath spoken unto them by the hand of Moses. (Lev. 10:11)
7. The Lord commanded me at that time to teach you statues and judgments. (Deu. 4:14)
8. Thou shalt teach them diligently unto thy children. (Deu. 6:7)
9. Do according to all that the priests the Levites shall teach you. (Deu. 24:8)
10. Set magistrates and judges, which may judge all the people that are beyond the river, all such as know the laws of thy God; and teach ye them that know them not. (Ezra 7:25)
11. And thou hast also appointed prophets to preach of thee at Jerusalem. (Neh. 6:7)
12. Teach me, and I will hold my tongue: and cause me to understand wherein I have erred. (Job 6:24)
13. Shall not they teach thee, and tell thee, and utter words out of their heart. (Job 8:10)
14. They shall teach thee. (Job 12:7)
15. It shall teach thee. (Job 12:8)

16. Shall any teach God knowledge? (Job 21:22)
17. I will teach you by the hand of God: that which is with the almighty will I not conceal. (Job 27:11)
18. Days should speak, and multitude of years should teach wisdom. (Job 32:7)
19. Hearken unto me: hold thy peace, and I shall teach thee wisdom. (Job 33:33)
20. That which I see not teach thou me: if I have done iniquity, I will do no more. (Job 34:32)
21. Teach us what we shall say unto him; for we cannot order our speech by reason of darkness. (Job 37:19)
22. Show me thy ways, O Lord; teach me thy paths. (Ps. 25:4)
23. Teach me: for thou art the God of my salvation. (Ps. 25:5)
24. Good and upright is the Lord: therefore will he teach sinners in the way. (Ps. 25:8)
25. The meek will he teach his way. (Ps. 25:9)
26. What man is he that feareth the Lord? Him shall he teach in the way that he shall choose. (Ps. 25:12)
27. Teach me thy way, O Lord and lead me in a plain path, because of mine enemies. (Ps. 27:11)
28. I will instruct thee and teach thee in the way which thou shalt go. (Ps. 32:8)
29. I will teach you the fear of the Lord. (Ps. 34:11)
30. Thy right hand shall teach thee terrible things. (Ps. 45:4)
31. Then will I teach transgressors thy ways: and sinners shall be converted unto thee. (Ps. 51:13)
32. Teach me thy way, O Lord; I will walk in thy truth: unite my heart to fear they name. (Ps. 86:11)
33. Teach his senators wisdom. (Ps. 105:22)
34. Teach me good judgment and knowledge. (Ps. 119:66)
35. Teach me to do thy will; for thou art my God: thy spirit is good. (Ps. 143:10)
36. Teach a just man, and he will increase in learning. (Prov. 9:9)
37. He will teach us of his ways, and we will walk in his paths;. (Isa. 2:3)

38. Whom shall he teach knowledge? And whom shall he make to understand doctrine? Them that are weaned from the milk, and drawn form the breasts. (Isa. 28:9)
39. For his God doth instruct him to discretion, and doth teach him. (Isa. 28:26)
40. The spirit of the Lord God is upon me; because the Lord hath anointed me to preach good tidings unto the meek. (Isa. 61:1)
41. Hear the word of the Lord, O ye women, and let your ear receive the word of his mouth, and teach your daughters wailing. (Jer. 9:20)
42. They shall teach my people the difference between the holy and profane, and cause them to discern between the unclean and the clean. (Ezek. 44:23)
43. Arise, go unto Nineveh, that great city, and preach unto it the preaching that I bid thee. (Jonah 3:2)
44. From that time Jesus began to preach, and to say, Repent: for the kingdom of heaven is at hand. (Matt. 4:17)
45. And as ye go, preach, saying, The kingdom of heaven is at hand. (Matt. 10:7)
46. The poor have the gospel preached to them. (Matt. 11:5)
47. This gospel of the kingdom shall be preached in all the world for a witness unto all nations. (Matt. 24:14)
48. He departed thence to teach and to preach in their cities. (Matt.11:1)
49. Preach the baptism of repentance for the remission of sins. (Mk. 1:4)
50. Preached, saying, There cometh one mightier than I after me. (Mk. 1:7)
51. Let us go into the next towns that I may preach there also. (Mk. 1:38)
52. He preached in their synagogues throughout all Galilee, and cast out devils. (Mk. 1:39)
53. He preached the word unto them. (Mk. 2:2)
54. They went out, and preached that men should repent. (Mk. 6:12)

55. Wheresoever this gospel shall be preached throughout the whole world. (Mk. 14:9)
56. Go ye into all the world, and preach the gospel to every creature. (Mk. 16:15)
57. They went forth, and preached every where, the Lord working with them, and confirming the word with signs following. (Mk. 16:20)
58. Many other things in his exhortation preached he unto the people. (Lk. 3:18)
59. The spirit of the Lord is upon me, because he hath anointed me to preach the gospel to the poor; he hath sent me to heal the brokenhearted, to preach deliverance to the captives, and recovering of sight to the blind, to set at liberty them that are bruised. (Lk. 4:18)
60. To preach the acceptable year of the Lord. (Lk. 4:19)
61. I must preach the kingdom of God to other cities also: for therefore am I sent. (Lk. 4:43)
62. He preached in the synagogues of Galilee. (Lk. 4:44)
63. He sent them to preach the kingdom of God, and to heal the sick. (Lk. 9:2)
64. Let the dead bury the dead: but go thou and preach the kingdom of God. (Lk. 9:60)
65. Since that time the kingdom of God is preached, and every man presseth into it. (Lk. 16:16)
66. And that repentance and remission of sins should be preached in his name among all nations. (Lk. 24:47)
67. Being grieved that thy taught the people, and preached through Jesus the resurrection from the dead. (Acts 4:2)
68. When they believed Philip preaching the things concerning the kingdom of God, and the name of Jesus Christ, they were baptized, both men and women. (Acts 8:12)
69. When they had testified and preached the word of the Lord. (Acts 8:25)
70. Then Philip opened his mouth, and began at the same scripture, and preached unto him Jesus. (Acts 8:35)

71. Passing through he preached in all the cities. (Acts 8:40)
72. And straightway he preached Christ in the synagogues, that he is the Son of God. (Acts 9:20)
73. He commanded us to preach unto the people, and to testify that it is he which was ordained of God to be the Judge of quick and dead. (Acts 10:42)
74. When they were at Salamis, they preached the word of God in the synagogues of the Jews. (Acts 13:5)
75. We also are men of like passions with you, and preach unto you that ye should turn from these vanities unto the living God. (Acts 14:15)
76. Let us go again and visit our brethren in every city where we have preached the word of the Lord. (Acts 15:36)
77. They were forbidden of the Holy Ghost to preach the word in Asia. (Acts 16:6)
78. Paul preached unto them. (Acts 20:7)
79. I am ready to preach the gospel to you that are at Rome also. (Rom. 1:15)
80. The word is nigh thee, even in thy mouth, and in thy heart: that is, the word of faith, which we preach. (Rom. 10:8)
81. How shall thy believe in him of whom thy have not heard? And how shall thy hear without a preacher? (Rom. 10:14)
82. How shall they preach, except they be sent? (Rom. 10:15)
83. I have fully preached the gospel of Christ. (Rom. 15:19)
84. So Have I strived to preach the gospel. (Rom. 15:20)
85. For Christ sent me not to baptize, but to preach the gospel. (1 Cor. 1:17)
86. Even so hath the Lord ordained that they which preach the gospel should live of the gospel. (1 Cor. 1:14)
87. For though I preach the gospel, I have nothing to glory of: for necessity is laid upon me; yea, woe is unto me, if I preach not the gospel. (1 Cor. 9:16)
88. When I peach the gospel, I may make the gospel of Christ without charge, that I abuse not my power in the gospel. (1 Cor. 9:18)
89. I declare unto you the gospel which I preached unto you, which also ye have received, and wherein ye stand. (1 Cor. 15:1)

90.   If you keep in memory what I preached unto you. (1 Cor. 15:2)
91.   Therefore whether it were I or they, so we preach, and so ye believed. (1Cor. 15:11)
92.   Now if Christ be preached that he rose from the dead, how say some among you that there is no resurrection of the dead. (1 Cor. 15:12)
93.   For we preach not ourselves, but Christ the Lord. (2 Cor. 4:5)
94.   To preach the gospel in the regions beyond you, and not to boast in another man's line of things made ready to our hand. (2 Cor. 10:16)
95.   If any man preach any other gospel unto you that that ye have received, let him be accursed. (Gal. 1:9)
96.   That I might preach him among the heathen. (Gal. 1:16)
97.   I went up by revelation, and communicated unto them that gospel which I preach among the Gentiles. (Gal. 2:2)
98.   Ye know how through infirmity of the flesh I preached the gospel unto you at the first. (Gal. 4:13)
99.   And came and preached to you which were afar off and to them that were nigh. (Eph. 2:17)
100. I should preach among the Gentiles the unsearchable riches of Christ. (Eph. 3:8)
101. Whom we preach, warning every man, and teaching every man in all wisdom; that we may present every man perfect in Christ Jesus. (Col. 1:28)
102. Preach the word; be instant in season, out of season; reprove, rebuke, exhort with all longsuffering and doctrine. (2 Tim.4:2)
103. For this cause was the gospel preached also to them that are dead, that thy might be judged according to men in the flesh, but live according to God in the spirit. (1 Pet. 4:6)
104. They to whom it was first preached entered not in because of unbelief. (Heb. 4:6)

SCRIPTURES FOR DELIVERANCE

1. Into your hand are they delivered. (Gen. 9:2)
2. When her days to be delivered were fulfilled, behold, there were twins in her womb. (Gen. 25:24)
3. Deliver me, I pray thee, from the hand of my brother. (Gen. 32:11)
4. So will I deliver you your brother, and ye shall traffic in the land. (Gen. 42:34)
5. And delivered our house. (Ex. 12:27)
6. I will deliver the inhabitants of the Land into your hand. (Ex. 23:31)
7. Fear him not: for I will deliver him, and all his people, and his land, into thy hand. (Deu. 3:2)
8. Thou shalt consume all the people which the Lord thy God shall deliver thee. (Deu. 7:16)
9. The Lord delivered unto me two tables of stone written with the finger of God. (Deu. 9:10)
10. The Lord your God will deliver it into your hand. (Josh. 8:7)
11. The Lord delivered all their enemies into their hand. (Josh. 21:44)
12. I will deliver him into thine hand. (Jud. 4:7)
13. Who shall deliver us out of the hand of these mighty Gods. (1 Sam. 4:8)
14. Phinehas wife, was with child, near to be delivered. (1 Sam. 4:19)
15. I will deliver thine enemy into thine hand. (1 Sam. 24:4)
16. Deliver me my wife Michal. (2 Sam. 3:14)

17. He delivered me from my strong enemy, for they were too strong for me. (2 Sam. 22:18)
18. He brought me forth also into a large place: he delivered me, because he delighted in me. (2 Sam. 22:20)
19. I was delivered of a child with her in the house. (1 Kng. 3:17)
20. Thou shalt deliver me thy silver and thy gold. (1 Kng. 20:5)
21. The Lord will surely deliver us. (2 Kng. 18:30)
22. The Lord saved them by a great deliverance. (1 Chron. 11:14)
23. The Lord delivered a great host into their hand. (2 Chron. 24:24)
24. They delivered the money that was brought into the house of God. (2 Chron. 34:9)
25. God hath delivered me to the ungodly, and turned me over into the hands of the wicked. (Job 16:11)
26. He shall deliver the island of the innocent: and it is delivered by the pureness of thine hands. (Job 22:30)
27. I delivered the poor that cried, and the fatherless, and him that had none to help him. (Job 29:12)
28. Then he is gracious unto him and saith, Deliver him from going down to the pit. (Job 33:24)
29. Then a great ransom cannot deliver thee. (Job 36:18)
30. Return, O Lord, deliver my soul; oh save me for thy mercies sake. (Ps. 6:4)
31. Lest he tear my soul like a lion, rending it in pieces, while there is none to deliver. (Ps. 7:2)
32. He delivered me from my strong enemy, and from them which hated me. (Ps. 18:17)
33. He brought me forth also into a large place; he delivered me, because he delighted in me. (Ps. 18:19)
34. Thou hast delivered me from the strivings of the people. (Ps. 18:43)
35. He delivered me from mine enemies: thou liftest me up above those that rise up against me. (Ps. 18:48)
36. They cried unto thee, and were delivered. (Ps. 22:5)
37. Deliver my soul from the sword. (Ps. 22:20)
38. Deliver me not over unto the will of mine enemies. (Ps. 27:12)

39. In thee, O Lord, do I put my trust; let me never be ashamed: deliver me in thy righteousness. (Ps. 31:1)
40. Bow down thine ear to me; deliver me speedily: be thou my strong rock. (Ps. 31:2)
41. Thou shalt compass me about with songs of deliverance. (Ps. 32:7)
42. A mighty man is not delivered by much strength. (Ps. 33:16)
43. I sought the Lord, and he heard me, and delivered me from all my fears. (Ps. 34:4)
44. Deliver me from all my transgressions: make me not the reproach of the foolish. (Ps. 39:8)
45. The Lord will deliver him in time of trouble. (Ps. 41:1)
46. Thou art my King, O God: command deliverance for Jacob. (Ps. 44:4)
47. Ye that forget God, lest I tear you in pieces, and there be none to deliver. (Ps. 50:22)
48. For he hath delivered me out of all trouble. (Ps. 54:7)
49. He hath delivered my soul in peace from the battle that was against me. (Ps. 55:18)
50. For thou hast delivered my soul from death: wilt not thou deliver my feet from falling. (Ps. 56:13)
51. Deliver me from the workers of iniquity. (Ps. 59:2)
52. That thy beloved may be delivered save with thy right hand, and hear me. (Ps. 60:5)
53. Deliver me out of the mire, and let me not sink: let me be delivered from them that hate me. (Ps. 69:14)
54. Make haste, O God to deliver me; make hast to help me, O Lord. (Ps. 70:1)
55. He shall deliver the needy when he crieth; the poor also, and him that hath no helper. (Ps. 72:12)
56. Deliver us, and purge away our sins, for thy name's sake. (Ps. 79:9)
57. He delivered them out of their distress. (Ps. 107:6)
58. And delivered them from their destruction. (Ps. 107:20)
59. That thy beloved may be delivered. (Ps. 108:6)

60. Deliver me from the oppression of man: so will I keep thy precepts. (Ps. 119:134)
61. Consider mine affliction, and deliver me: for I do not forget thy law. (Ps. 119:153)
62. Deliver me according to thy word. (Ps. 119:170)
63. I am brought very low: deliver me from my persecutors. (Ps. 142:6)
64. Send thine hand from above; rid me, and deliver me out of great waters. (Ps. 144:7)
65. Rid me, and deliver me from the hand of strange children, whose mouth speaketh vanity. (Ps. 144:11)
66. A crown of glory shall she deliver to thee. (Prov. 4:9)
67. The righteous is delivered out of trouble and the wicked cometh in his stead. (Prov. 11:8)
68. Through knowledge shall the just be delivered. (Prov. 11:9)
69. The seed of the righteous shall be delivered. (Prov. 11:21)
70. He that trusteth in his own heart is a fool: but whoso walketh wisely, he shall be delivered. (Prov. 28:26)
71. Now there was found in it a poor wise man, and he by his wisdom delivered the city. (Eccl. 9:15)
72. I had great bitterness: but thou hast in love to my soul delivered it from the pit of corruption. (Isa. 38:17)
73. Is my hand shortened at all, that it cannot redeem: or have I no power to deliver. (Isa. 50:2)
74. When thou criest, let thy companies deliver thee. (Isa. 57:13)
75. She was delivered of a man child. (Isa. 66:7)
76. I have delivered her into the hand of her lovers. (Ezek. 23:9)
77. They are all delivered unto death. (Ezek. 31:14)
78. She is delivered to the sword. (Ezek. 32:20)
79. He that taketh warning shall deliver his soul. (Ezek. 33:5)
80. I will deliver my flock from their mouth, that they may not be meat for them. (Ezek. 34:10)
81. Our God whom we serve is able to deliver us from the burning fiery furnace. (Dan. 3:17)
82. O Daniel, is thy God, whom thou servest continually, able to deliver thee from the lions. (Dan. 6:20)

83. Whosoever shall call on the name of the Lord shall be delivered. (Joel 2:32)
84. Upon mount Zion shall be deliverance. (Obad. 17)
85. He may be delivered from the power of evil. (Habak. 2:9)
86. Deliver thyself, O Zion, that dwellest with the daughter of Babylon. (Zech. 2:7)
87. Deliver us from evil: For thine is the kingdom, and the power, and the glory, for ever. (Matt. 6:13)
88. All things are delivered unto me of my father. (Matt. 11:27)
89. Who called his own servants, and delivered unto them his goods. (Matt. 25:14)
90. Now Elisabeth's full time came that she should be delivered; and she brought forth a son. (Lk.1:57)
91. He hath sent me to preach deliverance to the captives. (Lk. 4:18)
92. I have committed nothing against the people, yet was I delivered prisoner. (Acts. 28:17)
93. Now we are delivered from the law. (Rom. 7:6)
94. Who shall deliver me from the body of this death. (Rom. 7:24)
95. Who delivered us from so great a death, in whom we trust that he will yet deliver us. (2 Cor. 1:10)
96. The Lord shall deliver me from every evil work. (2 Tim. 4:18)
97. The Lord knoweth how to deliver the godly out of temptations. (2 Pet. 2:9)

SCRIPTURES FOR HEALING

1. Prayed unto God: and God healed. (Gen. 20:17)
2. I am the Lord that healeth thee. (Ex. 15:26)
3. He shall cause him to be thoroughly healed. (Ex. 21:19)
4. The scall is healed. (Lev. 13:37)
5. The plague healed. (Lev. 14:48)
6. Heal her now, O God. (Num. 12:13)
7. See now that I, even I, am he, and there is no god with me: I heal. (Deu. 32:39)
8. Ye shall be healed. (1 Sam. 6:3)
9. Thus saith the Lord, I have heard thy prayer, I have seen thy tears: behold, I will heal thee. (2 Kng. 20:5)
10. What shall be the sign that the Lord will heal me. (2 Kng. 20:8)
11. The Lord hearken to Hezekiah, and healed the people. (2 Chron. 30:20)
12. He shall be unto thee a restorer of thy life. (Ruth 4:15)
13. I am weak: O Lord, heal me; for my bones are vexed. (Ps. 6:2)
14. He restoreth my soul. (Ps. 23:3)
15. O Lord my God, I cried unto thee, and thou hast healed me. (Ps. 30:2)
16. Lord, be merciful unto me: heal my soul; for I have sinned against thee. (Ps. 41:4)
17. Restore unto me the joy of thy salvation. (Ps. 51:12)
18. He sent his word and healed them. (Ps.107:20)
19. He healeth the broken in heart, and bindeth up their wounds. (Ps. 147:3)
20. A time to heal; and a time to build up. (Eccl. 4:3)

21. He shall be entreated of them, and shall heal them. (Isa. 19:22)
22. The Lord healeth the stroke of their wound. (Isa. 30:26)
23. With his stripes we are healed. (Isa. 53:5)
24. I have seen his ways, and will heal him. (Isa. 57:18)
25. Saith the Lord; I will heal him. (Isa. 57:19)
26. Heal me, O Lord, and I shall be healed. (Jer. 17:14)
27. I will restore health unto thee and I will heal thee of thy wounds, saith the Lord. (Jer. 30:17)
28. O Virgin daughter of Zion: who can heal thee. (Lam. 2:13)
29. They shall be healed; and every thing shall live. (Ezek. 47:9)
30. Come, and let us return unto the Lord: for he hath torn, and he will heal us. (Hos. 6:1)
31. They knew not that I healed them. (Hos. 11:3)
32. Jesus healing all manner of sickness and all manner of disease among the people. (Matt. 4:23)
33. Jesus saith unto him, I will come and heal him. (Matt. 8:7)
34. Speak the word only, and my servant shall be healed. (Matt. 8:8)
35. He cast out the spirits with his word, and healed all that were sick. (Matt. 8:16)
36. Jesus said stretch forth thine hand, and his hand was restored whole as the other. (Mk. 3:5)
37. Restoreth all things. (Mk. 9:12)
38. They were healed. (Lk. 6:18)
39. He that was possessed of the devils was healed. (Lk. 8:36)
40. And healed all them that had need of healing. (Lk. 9:11)
41. Jesus rebuked the unclean spirit, and healed the child. (Lk. 9:42)
42. He took him, and healed him. (Lk. 14:4)
43. Jesus healed his son: he was at the point of death. (Jhn. 4:47)
44. They were healed every one. (Acts 5:16)
45. Healing all that were oppressed of the devil. (Acts 10:38)
46. He had faith to be healed. (Acts 14:9)
47. Paul entered in and prayed, and laid his hands on him and healed him. (Acts 28:8)
48. Came and were healed. (Acts 28:9)
49. Confess your faults one to another, and pray one for another, that ye may be healed. (Jms. 5:16)

50. By whose stripes ye were healed. (1 Pet. 2:24)
51. His deadly wound was healed. (Rev. 13:3)
52. Whose deadly wound was healed. (Rev. 13:12)

SCRIPTURES FOR PROSPERITY

1. Abram was very rich in cattle, in silver, and in gold. (Gen. 13:2)
2. I have made Abram rich. (Gen. 14:23)
3. The Lord hath prospered my way. (Gen. 24:56)
4. The Lord was with Joseph, and he was a prosperous man. (Gen. 39:2)
5. The Lord made all that he did to prosper in his hand. (Gen. 39:3)
6. That which he did, the Lord made it to prosper. (Gen. 39:23)
7. It is God that giveth power to get wealth. (Deu. 8:18)
8. Ye may prosper in all that ye do. (Deu. 29:9)
9. Then thou shalt make thy way prosperous and have good success. (Josh. 1:8)
10. Return with much riches unto your tents. (Josh. 22:8)
11. All the wealth God shall give Isreal. (1 Sam. 2:32)
12. The king will enrich him with great riches. (1 Sam. 17:25)
13. Thy wisdom and prosperity exceedeth the fame which I heard. (1 Kng. 10:7)
14. He prospered whithersoever he went forth. (2 Kng. 18:7)
15. I will give thee riches, and wealth, and honour. (2 Chron. 1:12)
16. He hath given us rest on every side, So they built and prospered. (2 Chron. 14:7)
17. He did it with all his heart, and prospered. (2 Chron. 31:21)
18. Hezekiah had exceeding much riches and honour. (2 Chron. 32:27)
19. Hezekiah prospered in all his works. (2 Chron. 32:30)
20. This work goeth fast on, and prospereth in their hands. (Ezra 5:8)

21. They prospered through the prophesying of the prophet. (Ezra 6:14)
22. The God of heaven, he will prosper us. (Neh. 2:20)
23. They spent their days in wealth. (Job 21:13)
24. I rejoiced because my wealth was great. (Job 31:25)
25. They shall spend their days in prosperity and their years in pleasures. (Job 36:11)
26. Let the Lord be magnified, which hath pleasure in the prosperity of his servant. (Ps. 35:27)
27. Be not thou afraid when one is made rich. (Ps. 49:16)
28. If riches increase, set not your heart upon them. (Ps. 62:10)
29. Thou broughtest us out into a wealthy place. (Ps. 66:12)
30. They increase in riches. (Ps. 73:12)
31. Wealth and riches shall be in his house. (Ps. 112:3)
32. O Lord, I beseech thee, send now prosperity. (Ps. 118:25)
33. Peace be within thy walls, and prosperity within thy palaces. (Ps. 122:7)
34. In her left hand riches and honour. (Prov. 3:16)
35. Riches and honour are with me. (Prov. 8:18)
36. The hand of the diligent maketh rich. (Prov. 10:4)
37. The blessings of the Lord, it maketh rich, and he addeth no sorrows with it. (Prov. 10:22)
38. Strong men retain riches. (Prov. 11:16)
39. The rich hath many friends. (Prov. 14:20)
40. Wealth maketh many friends. (Prov. 19:4)
41. The rich ruleth over the poor. (Prov. 22:7)
42. Every man also to whom God hath given riches and wealth. (Eccl. 5:19)
43. A man to whom God hath given riches, wealth, and honour. (Eccl. 6:2)
44. In the day of prosperity be joyful. (Eccl. 7:14)
45. My hand hath found as a nest the riches of the people. (Isa. 10:14)
46. They will carry their riches upon the shoulders of young asses. (Isa. 30:6)

47. I will give thee the treasures of darkness, and hidden riches of secret places. (Isa. 45:3)
48. I have brought him, and he shall make his way prosperous. (Isa. 48:15)
49. The pleasure of the Lord shall prosper in his hand. (Isa. 53:10)
50. No weapon that is formed against thee shall prosper. (Isa. 54:17)
51. It shall prosper in the thing whereto I sent it. (Isa. 55:11)
52. Ye shall eat the riches of the Gentiles. (Isa. 61:6)
53. They are become great, and waxen rich. (Jer. 5:27)
54. Yet they prosper. (Jer. 5:28)
55. I spake unto thee in thy prosperity. (Jer. 22:21)
56. They shall fear and tremble for all the goodness and for all the prosperity that I procure unto it. (Jer.33:9)
57. Arise, get you up unto the wealthy nation. (Jer. 49:31)
58. Thou didst prosper into a kingdom. (Ezek. 16:13)
59. Thy wisdom and thy understanding hast gotten thee riches, gold and silver. (Ezek. 28:4)
60. By thy great wisdom and by thy traffic hast thou increased thy riches. (Ezek. 28:5)
61. This Daniel prospered in the reign of Darius, and in the reign of Cyrus the Persian. (Dan. 6:28)
62. It practiced, and prospered. (Dan. 8:12)
63. He shall cause craft to prosper in his hand. (Dan. 8:25)
64. The fourth shall be far richer than they all. (Dan. 11:2)
65. Then shall he return into his land with great riches. (Dan. 11:28)
66. I am become rich. (Hos. 12:8)
67. The seed shall be prosperous. (Zech. 8:12)
68. Blessed be the Lord; for I am rich. (Zech. 11:5)
69. Many that were rich cast in much. (Mk 12:41)
70. He was very rich. (Lk. 18:23)
71. Ye know that by this craft we have our wealth. (Acts 19:25)
72. I might have a prosperous journey by the will of God to come unto you. (Rom. 1:10)
73. The same Lord over all is rich unto all that call upon him. (Rom. 10:12)

74. Now ye are full, now ye are rich. (1 Cor. 4:8)
75. God hath prospered him. (1 Cor. 16:2)
76. Making rich; as having nothing, and yet possessing all things. (2 Cor. 6:10)
77. He was rich, yet for your sakes he became poor, that ye through his poverty might be rich. (2 Cor. 8:9)
78. I wish above all things that thou mayest prosper and be in health, even as thy soul prospereth. (3 Jhn. 2)
79. I know thy works, and tribulation, and poverty, but thou art rich. (Rev. 2:9)
80. I am rich, and increased with goods, and have need of nothing. (Rev. 3:17)
81. I counsel thee to buy of me gold tried in the fire, that thou mayest be rich. (Rev. 3:18)

SCRIPTURES FOR MEN

1. A wise man will hear and increase learning and a man of understanding wisdom. (Prov. 1:5)
2. Put them in fear, O Lord: that the nations may know themselves as to be but men. (Ps. 9:20)
3. What is man that thou art mindful of him? And the son of man, that thou visitest him? (Ps. 8:4)
4. Man goeth forth unto his work and to his labour until the evening. (Ps. 104:23)
5. Lord, what is man, that thou takest knowledge of him, that thou makest account of him? (Ps. 144:3)
6. What is man that thou shouldest magnify him and set thine heart upon him? (Job 7:17)
7. How should man be just with God. (Job 9:2)
8. What is man, that he should be clean, which is born of a woman be righteous? (Job 15:14)
9. Unto man he said the fear of the Lord is wisdom and departing from evil is understanding. (Job 28:28)
10. Man's going are of the Lord; how can a man then understand his own way? (Prov. 20:24)
11. Surely I am more brutish than any man, and have not the understanding of a man. (Prov. 30:2)
12. Many will entreat the favour of the prince: and every man is a friend to him that giveth gifts. (Prov. 19:6)
13. A reproof entereth more into a wise man than an hundred stripes into a fool. (Prov. 17:10)
14. Reprove not a scorner, lest he hate thee: rebuke a wise man, and he will love thee. (Prov. 9:8)

15. Enter not into the path of the wicked, and go not in the way of evil men. (Prov. 4:14)
16. The wise man's eyes are in his head; but the fool walketh in darkness. (Ecc.2:14)
17. All the labour of man is for his mouth, and yet the appetite is not filled. (Ecc. 6:7)
18. God hath made man upright; but they have sought out many inventions. (Ecc. 7:29)
19. A wise man's heart is at his right hand; but a fool's heart at his left. (Ecc. 10:2)
20. To this man will I look, to him that is poor and of a contrite spirit, and trembleth at my word. (Isa. 66:2)
21. Let not the wise man glory in his wisdom, nor let the rich man glory in his riches. (Jer. 9:23)
22. Cursed be the man that trusth in man, and whose heart departeth from the Lord. (Jer. 17:5)
23. Man shall not live by bread alone but by every word that proceedeth out of the mouth of God. (Matt. 4:4)
24. I am a man under authority, having soldiers under me, and I say to this man go and he goeth. (Matt. 8:9)
25. If any man will come after me, let him take up his cross & follow me, let him deny himself. (Matt. 16:24)
26. But Peter took him up, saying, stand up; I myself also am a man. (Acts 10:26)
27. What man knoweth the things of a man, save the spirit of man which is in him? (1Cor. 2:11)
28. The natural man receiveth not the things of the Spirit of God: for they are foolishness to him. (1Cor. 2:14)
29. The first man is of the earth, earthy: the second man is the Lord from heaven. (1 Cor. 15:47)
30. Our outward man perish, yet the inward man is renewed day by day. (2 Cor.4:16)
31. If any man be in Christ, he is a new creature: old things are passed away; all things are new. (2 Cor. 5:17)
32. If any man preach any other gospel unto you than that ye have received, let him be accursed. (Gal. 1:9)

33. Let every man prove his own work, and then shall he have rejoicing in himself alone. (Gal. 6:4)
34. For every man shall bear his own burden. (Gal. 6:5)
35. Be not deceived: God is not mocked: for whatsoever a man soweth, that shall he reap. (Gal. 6:7)
36. Put off the former conversation of the old man, which is corrupt according to deceitful lusts. (Eph. 4:22)
37. Put on the new man, which after God is created in righteousness and true holiness. (Eph. 4:24)
38. Let it be the hidden man of the heart, in that which is not corruptible. (1 Pet. 3:4)
39. The Lord is a man of war: the Lord is his name. (Ex. 15:3)
40. God is not a man that he should lie; neither the son of man, that he should repent. (Num. 22:19)
41. Except a man be born again, he cannot see the kingdom of God. (Jhn. 3:3)
42. I am the living bread from heaven: If any man eat of this bread, he shall live for ever. (Jhn. 6:51)
43. If any man will do his will, he shall know of the doctrine, if I speak of God or myself. (Jhn. 7:17)
44. Jesus stood and cried, saying, if any man thirst let him come unto me, and drink. (Jhn. 7:37)
45. Now if any man have not the Spirit of Christ, he is none of his. (Rom. 8:9)
46. No man shall take away from the word of God prophecy or from the things written. (Rev. 22:19)
47. Warning every man, and teaching every man in all wisdom, presentable perfect in Christ. (Col. 1:28)
48. Jesus crowned with glory and honour by the grace of God tasted death for every man. (Heb. 2:9)
49. The good man is perished out of the earth: and there is none upright among them. (Mich. 7:2)
50. O man of God, flee these things; and follow after righteousness, faith, and love. (1 Tim. 6:11)
51. That the man of God may be perfect thoroughly furnished unto all good works. (2 Tim. 3:17)

52. A man shall leave his mother and father and cleave unto his wife and be one flesh. (Gen. 2:24)
53. If I be a man of God let fire come down from heaven and consume thee and thy fifty. (2 kng. 1:10)
54. O my Lord, let the man of God which thou didst send come again unto us and teach us. (Jud. 13:8)

SCRIPTURES FOR WOMEN

1. The damsel was very fair to look upon, a virgin, neither had any man known her. (Gen. 24:16)
2. He shall take a virgin of his own people to wife. (Lev. 21:12)
3. Let there be sought for my lord the king a young virgin: and let her stand before the king. (1 Kng. 1:2)
4. Behold, a virgin shall conceive, and bear a son and shall call his name Emmanuel. (Isa. 7:14)
5. For as a young man marrieth a virgin, so shall thy sons marry thee. (Isa. 62:5)
6. Again I will build thee, and thou shalt be built, O virgin of Israel. (Jer. 31:4)
7. Then shall the virgin rejoice in the dance, for I will turn their mourning into joy & comfort. (Jer. 31:13)
8. There is differences also between a wife and a virgin. The unmarried careth for the Lord. (1 Cor. 7:34)
9. I have espoused you to one husband, that I may present you as a chaste virgin to Christ. (2 Cor. 11:2)
10. Do not prostitute your daughter, to cause her to be a whore; lest the land fall to whoredom. (Lev. 19:29)
11. A certain woman cast a piece of a millstone upon Abimelech's head, and all to brake his skull. (Jud. 9:53)
12. Draw thy sword, and slay me, that men say not of me, A woman slew him. (Jud. 9:54)
13. The angel appeared unto the woman, now thou art barren, but thou shalt conceive. (Jud. 13:3)
14. She had a garment of divers colours upon her. (2 Sam. 13:18)

15. I am a woman of a sorrowful spirit: but have poured out my soul before the Lord. (1 Sam. 1:15)
16. She obtained grace and favour in his sight more than all the virgins. (Esth. 2:17)
17. She shall be brought unto the king in raiment of needlework. (Ps. 45:14)
18. Draw me, we will run after thee: the king hath brought me into his chambers. (Songs 1:4)
19. My virgins and my young men are fallen by the sword. (Lam. 2:21)
20. Then shall the kingdom of heaven be likened unto ten virgins. (Matt. 25:1)
21. Then all those virgins arose, and trimmed their lamps. (Matt. 25:7)
22. Afterward came also the other virgins, saying, Lord, Lord, open to us. (Matt. 25:11)
23. These were redeemed from among men, being the first fruits unto God and to the Lamb. (Rev. 14:4)
24. And now, my daughter, fear not; I will do to thee all that thou requirest. (Ruth 3:11)
25. A virtuous woman is a crown to her husband. (Prov. 12:4)
26. Who can find a virtuous woman? For her price is far above rubies. (Prov. 31:10)
27. Many daughters have done virtuously, but thou excellest them all. (Prov. 31:29)
28. She will do him good and not evil all the days of her life. (Prov. 31:12)
29. The heart of her husband doth safely trust in her, so that he shall have no need of spoil. (Prov. 31:11)
30. Strength and honour are her clothing; and she shall rejoice in time to come. (Prov. 31:25)
31. She openeth her mouth with wisdom; and in her tongue is the law of kindness. (Prov. 31:26)
32. She looketh well to the ways of her household, and eateth not the bread of idleness. (Prov. 31:27)

33. Her children arise up, and call her blessed; her husband also, and he praiseth her. (Prov. 31:28)
34. Favour is deceitful, beauty is vain: but a woman that feareth the Lord, she shall be praised. (Prov. 31:30)
35. Give her of the fruit of her hands; and let her own works praise her in the gates. (Prov. 31:31)
36. Hail, thou that art highly favoured, the Lord is with thee: blessed are thou among women. (Lk. 1:28)
37. But this woman hath anointed my feet with ointment. (Lk. 7:46)
38. And Jesus said to the woman, Thy faith hath saved thee; go in peace. (Lk. 7:50)
39. Blessed art thou among women, and blessed is the fruit of thy womb. (Lk. 1:42)
40. Woman thou art loosed from thine infirmity. (Lk. 13:12)
41. The Lord make the woman that is come into thine house like Rachel and like Leah. (Ruth 4:11)
42. A gracious woman retaineth honour: and strong men retain riches. (Prov. 11:16)
43. As a jewel of gold in a swine's snout, so is a fair woman which is without discretion. (Prov. 11:22)
44. Every wise woman buildeth her house: but the foolish plucketh it down with her hands. (Prov. 14:1)
45. It is better to dwell in a corner of the housetop, than with a brawling woman in a wide house. (Prov. 21:9)
46. It is better to dwell in the wilderness, than with a contentious and an angry woman. (Prov. 21:19)
47. Let every man have his own wife, and let every woman have her own husband. (1 Cor. 7:2)
48. The head of every woman is the man; and the head of Christ is God. (1 Cor. 11:3)
49. The woman is the glory of a man. (1 Cor. 11:7)
50. I will greatly multiply thy sorrow and thy conception; in sorrow you shalt bring forth children. (Gen 3:16)
51. Behold now, I know that thou art a fair woman to look upon. (Gen. 12:11)

52. The woman shall not wear that which pertaineth unto a man. (Deu. 22:5)
53. I hate my life. (Job 7:16)

SCRIPTURES FOR CHILDREN

1. Thou shall have no other gods before me. (Ex. 20:3)
2. Honour thy father and thy mother: that thy days may be long upon the land. (Ex. 20:12)
3. A wise son maketh a glad father: but a foolish son is the heaviness of his mother. (Prov. 10:1)
4. A foolish son is grief to his father, and bitterness to her that bare him. (Prov. 17:25)
5. He that curseth father or mother, let him die the death. (Matt. 15:4)
6. He that sent me is with me: the father hath not left me alone; I do those things that please him. (Jhn. 8:29)
7. Ye do the deeds of your father. (Jhn. 8:41)
8. Then said Jesus to them. Peace be unto you: as my father hath sent me, even so send I you. (Jhn. 20:21)
9. Thou art my son, this day have I begotten thee. (Heb. 1:5)
10. God is the helper of the fatherless. (Ps. 10:14)
11. A father to the fatherless, is God in his holy habitation. (Ps. 68:5)
12. God defend the poor and fatherless: do justice to the afflicted and needy. (Ps. 82:3)
13. Leave thy fatherless children, I will preserve them alive. (Jer. 49:11)
14. For in God the fatherless findeth mercy. (Hos. 14:3)
15. Hear, O my son, and receive my sayings; and the years of thy life shall be many. (Prov. 4:10)
16. My son, keep thy father's commandment, and forsake not the law of thy mother. (Prov. 6:20)

17. A wise son heareth his father's instruction; but a scorner heareth not rebuke. (Prov. 13:1)
18. A fool despiseth his father's instruction: but he that regardeth reproof is prudent. (Prov. 15:5)
19. Even a child is known by his doings, whether his work be pure, and whether it be right. (Prov. 20:11)
20. Train up a child in the way he should go: and when he is old, he will not depart from it. (Prov. 22:6)
21. Foolishness is bound in the heart of a child; the rod of correction shall drive it far from him. (Prov. 22:15)
22. Withhold not correction from the child: for if thou beatest him with a rod, he shall not die. (Prov. 23:13)
23. Thou shalt beat him with the rod, and shalt deliver his soul from hell. (Prov. 23:14)
24. My son, if thine heart be wise, my heart shall rejoice. (Prov. 23:15)
25. The rod and reproof give wisdom: but a child left to himself bringeth his mother to shame. (Prov. 29:15)
26. Better is a poor and a wise child than an old and foolish king. (Eccl. 4:13)
27. A little child shall lead them. (Isa. 11:6)
28. Lord God! Behold I cannot speak: for I am a child. (Jer. 1:6)
29. Say not, I am a child: for thou shalt go to all that I shall send thee. (Jer. 1:7)
30. When I was a child, I spake as a child, I understood as a child, I thought as a child. (1 Cor. 13:11)
31. The wrath of God cometh on the children of disobedience. (Col. 3:6)
32. Children, obey your parents in the Lord: for this is right. (Eph. 6:1)
33. Honor thy father and mother, which is the first commandment with promise. (Eph. 6:2)
34. Children obey your parents in all things: for this is wellpleasing unto the Lord. (Col. 3:20)
35. Father's provoke not your children to anger, lest they be discouraged. (Col. 3:21)

36. My son, despise not thou the chastening of the Lord. (Heb. 12:5)
37. For whom the Lord loveth he chasteneth, and scourgeth every son. (Heb. 12:6)
38. If ye endure chastening, God dealeth with you as with sons. (Heb. 12:7)
39. If ye be without chastisement, then are ye bastards, and not sons. (Heb. 12:8)
40. Shall we not much rather be in subjection unto the Father of the spirits, and live? (Heb. 12:9)
41. Because ye are Sons, God hath sent forth the Spirit of his Son into your hearts. (Gal. 4:6)
42. Thou art no more a servant, but a son, and if a son, then heir of God through Christ. (Gal. 4:7)
43. We, like Isaac are children of promise. (Gal. 4:28)
44. Except ye be converted & be as little children, ye shall not enter into the kingdom of heaven. (Matt. 18:3)
45. Believe in the light, that ye may be the children of the light. (Jhn. 12:36)
46. Like as a father pitieth his children, so the Lord pitieth them that fear him. (Ps. 103:13)
47. They which are the children of the flesh, these are not the children of God. (Rom. 9:8)
48. There shall they be called the children of the living God. (Rom. 9:26)
49. Fear not little flock, because it is your father's good pleasure to give you the kingdom. (Lk. 12:32)
50. She saw that he was a goodly child, and hid him three months. (Ex. 2:2)
51. The child grew and the Lord blessed him. (Jud. 13:24)
52. The child did minister unto the Lord before the priest. (1Sam. 2:11)

Printed in the United States
72850LV00002B/94-96